O. S. Nock was born in 1905 and educated at Giggleswick School and the City and Guilds (Engineering) College. His entire professional career as an engineer was spent with the Westinghouse Brake and Signal Co. Ltd. where he became Chief Mechanical Engineer of the Signal and Mining Division. His work was mainly concerned with signalling and in 1969 he was elected President of the Institution of Railway Signal Engineers. A lifelong railway enthusiast, he has studied railways in all their aspects and travelled widely in the process. He has written more than sixty books, as well as contributing hundreds of articles to the technical and enthusiast press. His first-hand knowledge of locomotive working has been supplemented by many thousands of miles riding on the footplate with steam, and more recently, on diesels and electrics: in addition to a wealth of British and Continental experience of this kind, he has ridden extensively in Australia, South Africa and Canada.

'I am sure this will become one of the classics of British railway literature.' – *Model Railways*

'The author combines his analysis of speeds with his customary well-informed comment on locomotive design, railway history and personalities.' – *Railway World*

'Steam trains were capable of surprising turns of speed, many of them recorded in this busy and informative book.' – *Manchester Evening News*

'This makes great reading.' – *BBC*

Also available in the David & Charles Series

THE SOMERSET & DORSET RAILWAY – *Robin Atthill*

THE COUNTRYMAN WILD LIFE BOOK
Bruce Campbell (Editor)

THE LOST ROADS OF WESSEX – *C. Cochrane*

THE ANTIQUE BUYER'S DICTIONARY OF NAMES
A. W. Coysh

BUYING ANTIQUES – *A. W. Coysh and J. King*

INTRODUCTION TO INN SIGNS – *Eric R. Delderfield*

THE CAVAN AND LEITRIM RAILWAY
Patrick J. Flanagan

THE CANAL AGE – *Charles Hadfield*

HOLIDAY CRUISING ON INLAND WATERWAYS
Charles Hadfield and Michael Streat

THE SAILOR'S WORLD – *Captain T. A. Hampton*

OLD DEVON – *W. G. Hoskins*

LONDON'S TERMINI – *Alan A. Jackson*

LNER STEAM – *O. S. Nock*

SOUTHERN STEAM – *O. S. Nock*

THE COUNTY DONEGAL RAILWAYS
Edward M. Patterson

OLD YORKSHIRE DALES – *Arthur Raistrick*

RAILWAY ADVENTURE – *L. T. C. Rolt*

THE WEST HIGHLAND RAILWAY – *John Turner*

BRITISH STEAM SINCE 1900 – *W. A. Tuplin*

THE HIGHLAND RAILWAY – *H. A. Vallance*

The David & Charles Series

SPEED RECORDS ON BRITAIN'S RAILWAYS

A Chronicle of the Steam Era

O. S. NOCK
B SC, C ENG, FICE, FI MECH E

UNABRIDGED

PAN BOOKS LTD : LONDON

First published 1971 by David & Charles (Publishers) Ltd.
This edition published 1972 by Pan Books Ltd.
33 Tothill Street, London, SW1.

ISBN 0 330 23365 3

Printed in Great Britain by
Cox & Wyman Ltd, London, Reading and Fakenham

CONTENTS

LIST OF ILLUSTRATIONS

(between pages 104 and 105)

PREFACE

THE AGE of steam on British railways is now virtually ended. The time is thus appropriate for a reasoned appraisal of what the British steam railway locomotive has contributed to the cause of public transport in its lifetime of nearly one hundred and fifty years. This is a record of what has been achieved in the manner of train haulage at high speed, of out-and-out speed records, if not necessarily in the precise unequivocal form of an encyclopedia, yet certainly in a factual summary, together with some of the background to each successive performance. At the same time I have confined this commentary very largely to the mechanics of speed. In other works I have discussed very fully the situations in railway politics that led to the celebrated races to Scotland, in 1888 and 1895, and to a lesser extent the race from the west, in 1904. In this book I am concerned with the locomotives, the engineers whose designing and constructional skill enabled them to run as they did, and the drivers and firemen by whose endeavours they were kept at it for hours on end.

In view of the story of magnificent achievement that I have to tell I find it a little sad that in these days, when so many official attempts are being made to consolidate the 'image' of the newly electrified and dieselised railways of Great Britain, so frequently attempts are equally made to denigrate the age of steam, as if it were an episode best forgotten. Not many months ago a railwayman of very high standing, of whom I have generally the highest of opinions, was addressing a gathering of some hundreds of engineers and others connected with railway motive power, and to hammer home the advantages of the new power he told a story of the electrification of the former Great Central line between Manchester and Sheffield. The work was nearly completed and he spoke to the driver of one of the last steam-hauled mineral trains passing through Woodhead Tunnel, emphasising that they would not have that type of locomotive for much longer. The driver's reply had been brief and to the point: 'A blue-pencil good job too!'

It is perhaps typical of the 'new-image' propaganda that the story was related completely out of its true context. The working of heavy freight trains through the single track bores of the original Woodhead Tunnel was one of the grimmest tests ever set to British steam locomotive enginemen, and purely on the grounds of humanity I would have been one of the first to advocate the abolition of steam in such a place. It compared with the shorter, but even more diabolical, Devonshire Tunnel on the Somerset & Dorset line just outside Bath. To go through the latter bore on the second engine of a double-headed train, working hard on the 1 in 50 gradient, was one of the most unpleasant experiences I have ever endured on the footplate.

Woodhead Tunnel and still less Devonshire Tunnel have no place in the story of speed records, and in reverting to my present subject it is important in this preface to make some reference to the authorities whose documentation forms the basis of much of the data quoted in this book. In earlier days the writings of Charles Rous-Marten, the Rev W. J. Scott, and E. L. Ahrons provide much of the background. Rous-Marten wrote extensively in *The Engineer* before he inaugurated the famous series of articles on Locomotive Practice and Performance in the *Railway Magazine*. That series, continued for nearly fifty years by Cecil J. Allen, has recorded the great majority of the records made since 1910. Until a period marked roughly by the end of World War I there were very few persons compiling accurate records of train running; but the interest created by them has led to many enthusiasts following the cult, and becoming expert in logging train journeys. In recent years indeed so many runs have been logged that some that have record features may have escaped my notice. I know it is the experience of many authors that one has only to write a book on a particular subject to bring additional data to light!

O. S. Nock
November 1970

Silver Cedars
Higher Bannerdown
Batheaston
Bath

CHAPTER ONE

THE GAUGE TRIALS AND THE GREAT WESTERN

IN SEEKING to set on record some of the earliest speed achievements of British locomotives one is faced with a plethora, of statements handed down by word of mouth, together with the factual record of certain diligent and conscientious observers, who, however, were attempting to work to greater accuracy than the measuring facilities of the day would support. Consequently the early documentation in general contains much information that is vague and quite unreliable by modern standards, and is of interest purely as a collection of period pieces in the early history of the recording of locomotive performance. There is no doubt that the gauge controversy led to more consciousness of the need for accuracy in both observation and methods of recording, because the narrow gauge parties were faced by the neat and precise mind of Daniel Gooch. For several years before the setting up of the Gauge Commission Gooch was taking indicator diagrams from his locomotives, and he was able to produce some of these as evidence to the Commissioners to show that speeds of 60 to 65mph were of fairly common occurrence on the Great Western by the year 1845. Until then the only published information on British railway speeds was of certain records compiled by Whishaw as a result of observations on the Madeley Bank of the Grand Junction Railway in 1839.

The Madeley Bank, with its 3 miles descending at 1 in 177 and the long straight approach to Crewe that followed, has always been a tempting place for anyone having a mind to the making of speed records. In early days there were distance posts every 100 yards, and Whishaw attempted to record the passing times at every one of these posts to the nearest second. Now everyone who has made a regular practice of logging the running of express trains, and particularly of registering maximum and minimum speeds, knows that the faster one is travelling the more desirable it is to take speed readings over a longer distance than one quarter of a mile. My own practice for many years has been to change from quarter- to half-mile timings when the speed is around 80mph, and this with a stop-watch reading to one-tenth of a second. But here, in 1839, was an observer logging posts at 100-yard intervals to the nearest second. With four separate trains he claimed a speed of 68·18mph, which would involve the covering of 100 yards in exactly 3 seconds. There is no suggestion in such records as have been passed down to us that several 100-yard lengths were *each* covered at this same speed, merely that the highest speed otherwise recorded was 56¾mph. One cannot therefore accept that the 68·18mph is reliable.

From these early and unsuccessful attempts at speed recording one comes forward to the time when the Gauge Commission was sitting, and the result of Daniel Gooch's work at Swindon began to be apparent. It is somewhat significant that until Gooch was called to give evidence the question of engine performance had scarcely been touched upon. His evidence includes actual indicator diagrams taken from the Firefly class 2-2-2 engine *Ixion*, one of which was taken at a speed of 60mph in June 1845. Another engine of the class was quoted by Gooch as attaining 65mph with a load of 80 tons on a descending gradient of 1 in 880, between Swindon and Didcot, eastbound. The load was increased to 100 tons at Didcot, and a maximum of 60mph was attained east of Twyford. Following the evidence of Gooch and Brunel before the Commissioners, and the impressive details of performance that such evidence claimed, a good deal of the subsequent inquiry centred on the costs of running, and the relative safety of the broad and narrow gauge at high speed. After a great deal of argument from the narrow gauge parties Brunel was recalled, and on 22 November 1845 he suggested that some comparative tests should be made, under the supervision of an engineer appointed by the Commissioners. After a long discussion the Commissioners turned to Charles Saunders, who was present, and asked: 'This wish which you have expressed comes from the Great Western Company?'

Saunders replied: 'Yes, decidedly, we wish those opinions to be tested by facts and experiments and if possible, agreed experiments, with witnesses attending on each side, and seeing the weights and everything, so that everything should be marked down, and there should be no possibility of any dispute.'

On 2 December 1845 Brunel was again recalled, in company with the G.P. Bidder, a civil engineer who had been associated with the Stephensons since constructional days on the Liverpool and Manchester. Although he would have been assumed to have something of a narrow-gauge bias he was in fact an extremely fair-minded man, and proved most cooperative in arranging the trials.

Brunel at first proposed that the trials should be conducted, so far as the broad gauge was concerned, throughout between Paddington and Exeter.

To these suggestions Bidder added:

> With reference to the narrow gauge lines on which the experiments should be made, I should propose the York and Darlington and the Crewe and Manchester; if you took the line between London and Didcot, which is nearly a level line, that might be compared with the York and Darlington and with the Manchester and Crewe, but there is no narrow gauge line long enough to compare with the line from London to Exeter. If the Commissioners wished it, we would try the line between

London and Liverpool, but I do not think it would be a fair test.

Brunel replied:

Of course in a perfectly level line it is easier for the narrow gauge engines to approach our engines, but as the railways generally in England do not have, and are still less likely to have, gradients as good as those of the York and North Midland, it is very desirable to make experiments upon lines with steeper gradients; I should say that the Taunton and Exeter line would be very fair to make experiments upon as being a line of steep gradients. The Commissioners in comparing two lines can consider what allowances are to be made for differences of gradient. I would merely ask that some experiments should be made upon lines of steep gradients.

In the event however the trials were conducted between Darlington and York on the one hand, and between Paddington and Didcot on the other – both virtually level routes. Knowing that somewhat feeble locomotives were then working the London & Birmingham and the Grand Junction Railways, one can heartily agree with Bidder that a London–Liverpool run would not be a fair test against one of Gooch's Firefly 2-2-2s. It will be recalled that on the opening of the line to Exeter, on 1 May 1844, Gooch drove the *Actaeon* there and back himself, 387 miles with one engine in a single day, and made the return trip of 193½ miles in 4hr 40min – a*n overall* average, including stops, of 41·5mph. For the trials staged for the benefit of the Commissioners Gooch again used the *Ixion,* while the narrow gauge protagonists put forward one of the very latest Stephenson products, newly out of shops, the celebrated Great A. This was a rear-driver long-boilered type, which at the time was being strongly backed by Robert Stephenson himself.

One imagines that the comparative runs were organised

to indicate relative coal and water consumptions for equal work. Both *Ixion* and the Great A made average speeds of 46 to 47mph over their respective routes, with maximum speeds just in excess of 60mph. This was apparently well below the maximum capabilities of the Great Western locomotive. Both Brunel and Gooch went north to observe the trials of the Great A; they rode together on her footplate, and Gooch considered that at maximum speed she was right up to the limit for safety. He was so concerned about her bad riding that he persuaded Brunel not to make the return trip on her. Sir George Airy, the Astronomer Royal, who was one of the Gauge Commissioners, also had a trip on the Great A, and considered that her rough riding was due more to the quality of the track than to any inherent weakness in the design and construction of the locomotive. He reported some violent oscillation at a point somewhere near Alne. The Great A was of course the very latest thing on the narrow gauge, and was Robert Stephenson's pride and joy; but one feels that had the comparative trials been held a few years later there would have been several more orthodox narrow gauge engines that would have given the broad gauge a much closer run. It is of interest to recall that it was on the Great A that David Joy had his first footplate ride on a locomotive, from Leeds to Castleford. Not many years were to pass before his ever-famous *Jenny Lind* took the road; and what that type could do in the way of speed is told in the next chapter.

It is interesting and somewhat amusing to find how the results of the gauge experiments were regarded by some of the great authorities of fifty years ago. J. G. H. Warren, in his classic work *A Century of Locomotive Building*, strives hard to be impartial, while naturally having a strong allegiance to any product of Robert Stephenson & Co. E. L. Ahrons, in his equally famous work *The British Steam Railway Locomotive 1825–1925*, gives details of some additional runs that reveal an almost overwhelming superiority for the broad gauge, thus:

PADDINGTON & DIDCOT

Engine *Ixion*

Direction	*Trailing load tons*	*Average speed mph*	*Trailing load tons*	*Average speed mph*
Down	81½	47·5	61	52·4
Up	81½	50	71	54·6

YORK & DARLINGTON

Engine *Great A*

Direction	*Trailing load tons*	*Average speed mph*	*Trailing load tons*	*Average speed mph*
Down and Up	80	43¼	50	47

Apparently separate records were not kept for the two directions of running between York and Darlington, though here again as between Paddington and Didcot the slight gradient would favour the up direction.

At the moment I am concerned with the Great Western, which despite the efforts of the narrow gauge was making nearly all the running in the 1840s. In the year after the lengthy sittings of the Gauge Commissioners, in 1846, the Great Western pushed their advantage home in a very striking manner, yet in a way completely unaccompanied by any publicity. So much had been said during the various interrogations about the dangers of high speed that one imagines Gooch felt that his continued experiments and trials with his dynamometer car had best be kept fairly quiet for the time being. So far as size and tractive power was concerned the Great Western had leapt ahead of the Great A. Even while the Gauge Commission was still in session the directors had given Gooch authority to built 'a Colossal locomotive' and on 1 April 1846 the new 2-2-2 was steamed at Swindon. With cylinders 18in diameter by 24in stroke, and driving wheels 8ft diameter, she was far in advance of the Firefly class, which had 15¾in by 18in cylinders, and 7ft diameter driving wheels.

The first news the engineering world had of what was afoot on the Great Western came in June 1846, and then, in no less authoritative surroundings than the Institution of Civil Engineers. Wyndham Harding, one of the many eminent men who gave evidence before the Gauge Commissioners, read a paper 'On the Resistance to Railway Trains at Different Velocities'. Gooch did not take part in the oral discussion, which extended over meetings in three successive weeks; but on 9 June a letter from him was read, which included the following striking information about the running of the 'colossal locomotive', duly named *Great Western*:

'Within the last ten days I have made two experiments with an engine with 18in diameter, 24in stroke cylinders, and 8ft wheels. A gross load of 184 tons including the engine was taken at an average speed of 55mph with an evaporation of water equal to 5·32cu ft per mile, down a gradient averaging 4ft per mile; the steam being cut off at $\frac{15}{24}$ of the stroke ...'

A gradient of 4ft per mile is equal to 1 in 1320 and clearly indicates a run from Didcot to Paddington. Gooch adds, somewhat as an afterthought, that some of the carriages arrived with hot axles, although from the speed point of view this was much the same as the fastest *Ixion* run earlier that year. Then Gooch went on to reveal something, the significance of which was certainly not underlined at the time:

'On a second experiment with the same engine cutting off as before, at $\frac{15}{24}$, a gross load of 94 tons was carried at a speed of 67mph with a consumption of water equal to 4·5cu ft per mile, or a resistance of 34lb per ton; deducting 21lb per ton for gravity as it was on an ascending gradient. As I am making preparations for a series of experiments on this matter on a large scale, I offer no opinion on these facts, and shall be glad if they are of any use in the discussion on the subject.'

The fact that he had made a run from Paddington to Didcot at a start-to-stop average speed of 67mph, albeit with a light load, as early in railway history as 1846 was tossed almost casually into the forum of the Institution of Civil Engineers – not as a well-nigh sensational item in the development of railway transport. It may be questioned whether the statement can be accepted precisely at its face value. With anyone but Gooch I would be inclined to take it with the proverbial 'pinch of salt' myself. But Gooch had a sense of professional integrity and self discipline that was outstanding; and while he was ready enough to follow venturesome Brunel into any developments of great enterprise he could never be found guilty of polishing up the truth to suit his own arguments. When he and Brunel went north to witness some of the trials of the Great A engine between York and Darlington he was shocked to find that in certain circumstances that engine was being given a flying start, by starting her some little distance earlier so that she was passing the starting point at about 15mph instead of starting dead from it!

Apart from pure speed, Gooch had also been including in his series of experiments some long-distance running with the *Great Western*. According to E. L. Ahrons, who had his early training at Swindon in broad-gauge days, and who succeeded in unearthing a vast amount of most interesting early information, a test run was made on 1 June 1846 working the *Great Western* through from Paddington to Exeter and back on the same day. So far as mileage was concerned this was, of course, no advance upon what Gooch had achieved on the day of the opening of the line to Exeter two years earlier; but it was done at very much higher speed. In June

1846 the 387-mile round trip was made in a total running time of 419 minutes – 208 minutes going down and 211 minutes on the return. This gave an astonishing overall running average speed of 55·3mph. It is needless to add that the narrow gauge had nothing to touch this by that time, but it came too late to be considered by the Gauge Commissioners. In any case speed and haulage power of locomotives proved to be no more than a small consideration towards their final judgement upon railway gauges.

In her original form as a 2-2-2 the *Great Western* had a very short life. Not long after her record-breaking runs she broke her leading axle when running at speed near Shrivenham. Gooch thereupon lengthened the front framing, and distributed the weight upon two axles. Although nominally becoming a 4-2-2 the two leading axles were not formed into a bogie; both had bearings in the main frames. As such *Great Western* became the true prototype of the famous series of Gooch broad gauge eight-foot singles, though the first engine of the standard series, the *Iron Duke* completed in April 1847, had a more conventional firebox than the very picturesque copper-clad haystack type fitted on the *Great Western*.

The time now moves forward yet another year to April 1848, by which time Gooch had six of his standard eight-foot singles at work, in addition to the prototype *Great Western*. It was now his turn to make a major contribution to the proceedings of the Institution of Civil Engineers in the form of a paper entitled 'Observations on the Resistances to Railway Trains at Different Velocities'. The paper itself was largely concerned with a series of tests that Gooch had conducted with his dynamometer car, and concerned a special test train of six-wheeled passenger coaching stock, loaded with iron to represent an appropriate number of passengers. The tests described in the paper involved speeds up to 62mph and trailing loads up to 100 tons. The 'sprat' that eventually caught a historical 'mackerel' of the first magnitude was a suggestion in the paper that with the coaching stock then in use on the Great Western a speed of 55 to 60mph could be maintained by gravity alone on a descending gradient of 1 in 100. This brought a strong reply from Joseph Locke who said such an assertion was 'utterly at variance' with his experience. He stated that 'all experiments on the narrow gauge had proved that the uniform velocity varied from a minimum of 33 to a maximum of 36mph and there was no evidence to prove the possibility of attaining a higher velocity by the force of gravity alone'. What experiments Locke had conducted one cannot now conceive, because a maximum of 36mph would indicate a resistance of 22 to 23lb per ton at that speed. This question of the resistance of locomotives and coaching stock is of the utmost importance in the consideration of train speeds in relation to locomotive power, and thus to the whole theme of this book. These early assumptions have a far greater significance than the mere academic discussions between two rival groups of engineers.

Against the resistance of 22 to 23lb per ton at 36mph implied by Joseph Locke's remark, and presumably for engine and carriage together, the figure determined in the classic experiments of Sir John Aspinall on the Lancashire & Yorkshire Railway about the turn of the century gave around 9lb per ton at 36mph. Some thirty years later, with greatly improved coaching stock, F. C. Johansen devised a new formula which gave a resistance of no more than 7lb per ton at 36mph, while the latest British Railways tests quote no more than 5lb per ton at the same speed. Thus in equal circumstances on level track a locomotive could, for example, for the same output of power, pull four times the dead weight of modern stock to that with which Joseph Locke was concerned in 1848. Gooch on the other hand was on sure ground when he said that 55 to 60mph could be maintained by gravity alone on 1 in 100 descent. He had already measured the resistance of his trains, engines and carriages together, as around 25lb per ton at 60mph. Assuming the resistance of the engine to be roughly twice that of the carriages would indicate a coach resistance of about 16 or 17lb per ton. This would enable them to free-wheel down a gradient of 1 in 100 at about 55mph. In passing it is interesting to bear in mind the figures of Aspinall, Johansen and British Railways for coaching stock at 60mph at their respective periods, namely 15, 11·5, and 8·5lb per ton in calm weather. The latest figure is thus roughly half that of Gooch's carriages of 1848. These figures are very important when comparison comes to be made with modern runs, because some of the early records are often dismissed because they were made 'with a very light load'. The tonnage might be small but the trains pulled much more heavily than modern stock.

The discussion in Gooch's paper at the Institution of Civil Engineers extended over three evenings, and following Locke's remarks about speed on gradients Gooch prepared a statement in reply which included the most vital data on locomotive performance that had been published up to that time. Gooch said:

> A further check on experiments, made with the dynamometer, might be obtained from the consumption of water by the engine, in working the ordinary express trains. The tender held 1,600 gallons of water, and the express was in the constant practice of running the 53 miles to Didcot, without stopping, in 48 to 50 minutes, the general consumption of water being 1,500 to 1,550gal and the rise 118ft; the cylinders were 18in diameter and the steam was cut off at 15in, the full stroke being 24in.

Note first of all the astonishing statement from Gooch of all modest men, that the morning express from Paddington 'was in constant practice' of running to Didcot in 48 to 50min – maintaining in the process start-to-stop average speeds of 63½ to 66mph – in 1848! Then he went on:

> In one trip made a fortnight ago, with wheels 8ft in

> diameter, when Capt Simmonds and several engineers were present, an average speed of 67mph was obtained, with 1,550gal of water, which allowing one-sixth for back pressure would give 30lb per ton as the resistance of the engine and train weighing 115 tons on the level.

This remarkable performance, equalling that of the *Great Western* for speed but with a train heavier by 20 tons, showed a start-to-stop time of 47½min over the 53 miles from Paddington to Didcot, and the average speed remained an out-and-out British railway and world record for upwards of fifty years. The engine used on this occasion was the second of the standard eight-footers, the *Great Britain*. Over the years the basic facts of the run, the speed, the load and the engine concerned were passed down through generations of railwaymen, and when much closer scrutiny began to be made of train speeds and a race of scholarly and expert railway enthusiasts began to arise, this performance tended to be regarded more as a legend than as an actuality. Ahrons as a good Swindon man naturally heard all about it. To him, as an engineer keenly interested in both history and the actual performance, it was a 'legend' that more than ever excited his curiosity. He discovered that the man who fired the *Great Britain* on that occasion was still living; he sought him out, and talked frequently to him about the run. Ahrons afterwards commented that the fireman 'always maintained that it had been done as recorded, but as he was sixty-five to seventy years of age when the conversations took place his evidence is of doubtful value'. This was Ahrons's final summing up, in his book *The British Steam Railway Locomotive 1825-1925*, for he died soon after the text was published in serial form in *The Engineer* in 1925.

Then there was Charles Rous-Marten. In 1897, in one of the very first issues of the *Railway Magazine*, he wrote an article entitled 'Some Railway Myths'. It opened in characteristic style:

> At first sight it may seem not a little strange that such essentially prosaic and scientific things as railways should be able to produce any 'myths' at all. But it must be remembered that the vast possibilities of railway locomotion have a tendency to appeal to the imagination of marvel-lovers, and imagination of that sort is apt to clamour for the out-marvelling of marvels. Hence have arisen the wondrous tales of manifest impossibilities which have been current ever since railways were given to a grateful world.

He then went on to relate with the utmost relish the story of how Brunel once went from London to Bristol, light-engine in the even hour, and the fantasy, related at the time of the final abolition of the broad gauge, that the Gooch eight-footers 'frequently ran the twelve miles from Bath to Bristol in eight minutes'! But then he went on:

> There is another tale about an ancient feat on the Great Western, which has a good deal more of genuine basis than most of the others, but which, nevertheless, has embodied some manifest exaggeration, and, I suspect, more which can only be guessed at.

He then quotes the details that I have already discussed, and continues:

> How then, it will be asked, did the report originate? I understand that the time was taken from the *Guard's Journal.* I would not say one word to disparage the accuracy with which guards keep their books. Generally they keep them with scrupulous care and accuracy. To this I can testify after close comparison of returns. But precise timing is not their particular métier; and now and then, especially when a 'record' has to be established or 'broken', onc docs find a guard too enthusiastic or too much carried away by natural excitement to be entirely trustworthy.

He suggests that the Great Western guard on the run of 1848 may have looked at his watch just as Didcot came into sight, and in the thrill of what was obviously a supreme occasion jotted down that time, rather than the time when they actually stopped at the platform.

Thus one had, right down to the nineteen thirties, two of the greatest authorities in railway history both discounting the report of the *Great Britain* run of 1848. Nevertheless the story remained a very live one in Great Western circles, and it was not finally vindicated, or rather re-vindicated, until the year 1940, when a most scholarly analysis of the only data that really mattered – the Proceedings of the Institution of Civil Engineers – was made by Messrs J. T. Howard Turner and M. Grehan, in an article published in the *Railway Magazine* in February of that year. In addition to the facts published in 1848 by Daniel Gooch himself the joint authors sought to get additional corroboration from the Ministry of Transport. The Captain Simmons mentioned earlier as one of the distinguished visitors present on the 1848 occasion was an Inspecting Officer of Railways at the Board of Trade at that time; but no record of his participation survives. The chance that the time may have been inaccurately recorded can, I think, be discounted, both in respect of the starting and finishing time. Gooch had raised such strong objection to the 'fiddles' he had observed in this respect during the narrow gauge locomotive trials that he would hardly be likely to lay himself open to the same criticism, particularly with independent witnesses of the status of Captain Simmons present.

One can therefore set down in confidence that the first really high speed run to be authenticated, to the degree displayed in the Proceedings of Civil Engineers, can be credited to the Great Western. One must also bear in mind that it had been closely paralleled in 1846 on one of the earliest runs of the *Great Western* in her 2-2-2 condition, though with a lighter load. Again from Gooch's own words that 47½min run in 1848 does not appear to have been regarded as anything very much out of the ordinary, when 'the express was in the constant practice of running the 53 miles to Didcot, without stopping, in 48 to 50min'. Thus the record average speed, on the special trip, is established on Gooch's testimony at 67mph. One is, of course, intrigued to know what the intermediate running was like, but if, with a relatively light load, the first three miles had taken four minutes, and the last two, two minutes, that would leave 41½minutes for the intervening 48 miles, showing an average of 69½mph. This is quite feasible, and excellent work for the period.

One is naturally curious to know what maximum speeds were obtained by the Gooch eight-footers on the 1 in 100 bank between Wootton Bassett and Dauntsey, and down through the Box Tunnel. The most generally accepted performance, contemporary with the London–Didcot record run, occurred when Brunel and Gooch were together testing the eight-footers when new. Charles Sacré, who later became Locomotive Superintendent of the Manchester, Sheffield and Lincolnshire Railway, was on the Great Western at the time, and was present at the trials. Three different eight-footers were used, and each was driven flat out for a maximum speed. These engines were the *Iron Duke*, the *Courier* and the *Great Britain*, and they gave fairly consistent results. With the dynamometer car a maximum speed of 78mph was secured near Dauntsey, and this remained the authenticated British railway maximum speed for many years. The exciting times following the sittings of the Gauge Commission gave place, after 1852, to years of depression, and train service deceleration on the Great Western. The torch blazing the way towards higher speed running passed to other hands, and did not eventually return to the Great Western for over fifty years.

CHAPTER TWO

NARROW GAUGE: 1848 TO THE TRENT

MESSRS ROBERT STEPHENSON & Co supplied six of their long-boilered 4-2-0s to the London & North Western Railway in 1846–7. These engines had 7ft diameter driving wheels, but were otherwise similar to long-boilered engines built by the manufacturers under the Stephenson patent for the design. The old records show that at one time there were thirty-nine of them working on the Southern Division, and they were for a time the crack express engines of the line. The ones built by Stephenson & Co themselves, with a further two added in 1848, were however the only ones to have 7ft driving wheels. The others were all 6ft 6in. There is a special reason for mentioning the 7ft Stephensons, for one of them was concerned in the making of an unusually fast run in May 1847. In the previous July J. E. McConnell had become Locomotive Superintendent of the Southern Division of the LNWR and he was about the last man to stand by and let the Great Western claim all the speed honours. A special train having been chartered by an eminent party bound for Chester Races, including Lord George Bentinck, McConnell saw to it that the 'racing' began long before they reached Chester! Although the load was only light – five carriages – he put on one of the Stephenson 7ft 4-2-0s, No 157, and rode himself on the footplate, having with him a certain Mr Winter, who is described as the Superintendent of Mr Stephenson's patent engines.

At that time the journey had to be made via Birmingham, and a report in the *Newcastle Chronicle* of 7 May 1847 states that the 112 miles between Euston and Birmingham

(Curzon Street) were covered in two hours and thirty minutes. But the running time did not exceed the level two hours, because the train was stopped four times for signal delays, in addition to the customary stop at Wolverton to change engines. The report does not give the actual start-to-stop time from Euston to Wolverton, except to mention that the last 21 miles, downhill from Tring, were covered in 21 minutes. One must however treat with some reserve the claim that a maximum of 75mph was attained in the process. At Wolverton what is described as one of the 'ordinary' patent engines, No 157, was replaced by a new three-cylinder 4-2-0. This presumably was on loan to the LNWR. There does not appear to be evidence that one of these three-cylinder engines was ever taken into stock. The original engine of the type was one built in 1847 for the Newcastle & Darlington Junction Railway, and it may well have been this very engine that was used on the LNWR on this special occasion.

The three-cylinder engine did very well, covering the first 41 miles, from Wolverton to the outskirts of Coventry, in 42 minutes. There it was stopped because there was another train ahead; but the total running time from Euston to Curzon Street was, as previously mentioned, no more than 120 minutes indicating a running average of 56mph. The maximum speed claimed for the three-cylinder engine was 64mph. This is quite reasonable in view of the good start-to-stop run from Wolverton to Coventry. Nevertheless it is evident that these three-cylinder engines did not come up to expectations. J. G. H. Warren records that only two of them were built. Stephensons followed up their long-boiler predilections with a design having a pair of carrying wheels under the firebox, changing the locomotive into a 4-2-2, presumably to secure greater steadiness in running. Two of these engines were supplied to the London & North Western Southern Division in 1848; but it is significant that McConnell, having had experience of these 'patent' engines and also of the giant Crampton engine *Liverpool*, went in for a very simple, orthodox design when it came to building engines of his own at Wolverton Works. It is not without further significance in this direction that in 1848 the LNWR had purchased a couple of Jenny Lind 2-2-2s from E. B. Wilson. My own guess would be that these latter were easily the most reliable express locomotives then working on the Southern Division.

Mention of the Jenny Lind type, 2-2-2 with outside bearings for the leading and trailing wheels but inside bearings for the driving axle, and the year 1848 leads on to another special occasion on which some fast running was made. It was a time of great political unrest. Lord John Russell the great reformer was Chancellor of the Exchequer and great excitement centred on his Budget speech in February 1848. *The Times*, thundering for reform, was so anxious to get full details of the speech to Scotland as quickly as possible that arrangements were made with the newsagents W. H. Smith & Son to charter a special train, leaving Euston at 5.35am on the morning of 19 February. No records have been handed down of the type of locomotives used on the LNWR but at that period in history they would almost certainly have been of the 4-2-0 long-boilered class. Wolverton, 52·4 miles, was reached in exactly an hour, and the average speed over the continuation run to Rugby was 51½mph. These performances were nothing special having regard to the fact that the load was a very light one, even for the standards of those days. At Rugby the Midland took over, for the west coast route to Glasgow was not then complete. A Sharp 2-2-2, with outside bearings throughout, 16in by 20in cylinders, and 5ft 6in driving wheels, took the train on from Rugby to Derby via Leicester at an average speed of 52½mph.

Then at Derby one of the Jenny Linds took over, and she went up the North Midland line in great style. There did not exist in those days the numerous speed restrictions for colliery subsidences, and the 63·6 miles from Derby to Altofts Junction were covered in 68 minutes, start-to-stop, an average speed of 56mph. Altofts Junction, north of Normanton, is the point of divergence of the York & North Midland Railway. It is interesting to find that engines were changed there, instead of at Normanton station. Once off Midland metals the pace slowed down a good deal, and the overall average was brought down considerably because the parcels of newspapers had to be conveyed across the rivers at Newcastle and Berwick by road. At that time the railway bridges over the Tyne and the Tweed were not completed. The total running time by train over the 471 miles from London to Glasgow by this route was 752 minutes, an average of 37½mph. In view of the fine averages, all above 50mph, made on the LNW and Midland sections of the journey this suggests a very marked falling off in standards after Altofts Junction. The newspapers reached Glasgow in 10hr 22min from London.

It was at this stage in railway history that the ambitions of management and the prowess of locomotive engineers began to over-reach themselves. The beginning of the 1850s saw many locomotives at work in Great Britain that were capable of running at 65 to 70mph. Some, when pressed, could run up to about 75; but other factors in train working had not progressed so fast as the techniques of locomotive design. First and foremost there was the quality of the rails and of the road bed. Track maintenance was proving an expensive item. The relatively soft wrought-iron rails wore quickly, and such devices as the doubleheaded rail that was intended to be turned upside down when the upper surface had worn did not work out as intended. Good ballasting, even if its importance was appreciated, was a thing that could not be afforded in many a civil engineer's budget, and the quality of the track naturally precluded any regular running at the maximum speeds of which the locomotives were capable. Then there was the vital matter of brakes. In these days it is incredible to recall that until the 1870s it was the universal practice to fit *no brakes at all* on to tender locomotives. There was no retarding power except the hand-operated brakes on the tenders. Some locomotive engineers expressed objection to fitting engine brakes because of the torsional stresses set up in the driving axles. Signalling was also in its infancy, and yet it is on record that the directors of the London & North Western Railway announced their intention of running express trains between London and Birmingham in the even-two hours as early as 1852.

McConnell himself was ready enough to 'have a go'. He had a dashing, sport-loving temperament that revelled in any such challenge, and he was already well equipped with first-class locomotives. Out of his early experiences with the puny little Burys, patent long-boilered Stephensons and two Cramptons had been born the ultra-simple Bloomer 2-2-2s. While some engineers had struggled to keep the centre of gravity low to get smooth and steady riding, McConnell went to the opposite extreme in placing a large boiler over the driving axle of 7ft wheels. Furthermore, instead of bunching the wheels together at the rear end as in the Stephenson long-boilered type, he used a relatively long wheelbase. The result was an engine that, to quote David Joy, 'rode like a swing', and was easy on the track in consequence. These engines were also very powerful, because McConnell went to the high boiler pressure, for the year 1851, of 150lb per sq in. The 7ft Bloomers were really splendid engines, and it is a pity that track and other conditions prevented any demonstration of what they could do in the way of high speed. Against the two-hour London–Birmingham project, however, McConnell felt that something even larger and more powerful was necessary. The outcome was his own Patent locomotive; a 7ft 6in 2-2-2, in complete contrast to the Bloomers in that outside bearings were provided for all the wheels. They were extremely large engines for the day, and had a grate area of no less than 23½sq ft. Not a great deal is known about the general work of these engines, but one of them, No 300, featured in a comprehensive series of comparative trials run in 1853 between Northern and Southern Division locomotives of the LNWR between London and Birmingham.

The engines competing, other than the McConnell Patent 2-2-2, were a couple of Allan 2-2-2 6ft singles, an Allan 7ft single, and a McConnell 7ft Bloomer. So far as power output and speed were concerned it was, as might be expected, an absolute push-over for the McConnell engines. Whereas the maximum speed recorded with any of the Northern Division representatives was 51mph by the 7ft single No 290 *Rocket*, hauling a very light load of nine coaches weighing no more than 46 tons all told, McConnell's Patent engine No 300 reached a maximum speed of 54mph with no less than 34 coaches in tow, a trailing load of 171 tons. On the comparative Northern Division run with this load two 6ft singles had to be used, Nos 130 *Heron* and 291 *Prince of Wales*. The best the two engines together could do with the 34 coach train was 48mph and their consumption of coke was considerably greater than that of the one McConnell engine. The 7ft Bloomer included in the tests gave closely similar results to those from the Patent 2-2-2, though the former engine was not tested with any heavier load than 126 tons.

In the early 1850s, with the Great Western beginning to drop out of the picture due to economic reasons, two men seemed to be making the principal running for the future development of the British steam locomotive and its speed potential. Of these two McConnell was, of course, one, and the second was Archibald Sturrock. From its very inception the Great Northern had to fight against established railway interests, and from an early day there was full appreciation that this could most effectively be done by the speed of its trains. In 1850 they secured the services of a man whose temperament was much the same as that of McConnell: a man who 'thought big', who equally revelled in a sporting challenge, and who came to Doncaster fresh from the invaluable experience of working under Daniel Gooch at Swindon. Such a man was Archibald Sturrock, and in a short time he was instrumental in providing the Great Northern Railway with some locomotives of excellent capabilities.

Whereas the North Western, doubtless through its early associations, had previously been inclined towards the products of Robert Stephenson & Co, the Great Northern had formed an alliance with R. & W. Hawthorn, and some of the earliest engines introduced in the Sturrock regime were a development of the standard and very reliable Hawthorn 2-2-2 with outside frames throughout.

I have previously referred in this chapter to the difficulties in brake power and signalling that bedevilled railway working in the period of which I am now writing. There could be no more classic example of this than in the celebrated encounter between the Flying Scotsman and a goods train, on the Retford level crossing, when a speed record of a different kind was called for, and attained. Michael Reynolds, author of the classic work of the 1870s, *Locomotive Engine Driving*, tells the story under a sub-section dealing with instances in which a driver is called upon to display extreme presence of mind:

> The down Scotch express was going down Retford bank, signals all clear, when Oliver Hindley saw a train going east from Sheffield to Lincoln, which would meet him on the level crossing. He could not stop, and with that clear mind that is so marked in Englishmen in time of danger, he put on full steam, and sent Mr Sturrock's beautiful express engine clean through the goods train, scattering the trucks like match splinters, and carrying all safe. When asked about the matter Hindley said he could not keep clear, so he would clear away his obstruction. There is no doubt that, had he hesitated or feared, many lives would have been sacrificed. No 210 engine carried the dents and scars like an old warrior, and looked handsomer than ever for this brush with the enemy of express trains.

One can only add that a reconstruction of this affair would make an enlivening centre-piece for a television documentary!

Such a driver would obviously have been a man after Sturrock's own heart. He, like McConnell, was striding much ahead of the commercial needs of the day. Having achieved conspicuous success with the Large Hawthorn 2-2-2s, he got Hawthorns to build a remarkable engine, in his own words 'to prove to the directors of the Great Northern Railway that it was quite practicable to reach Edinburgh from Kings Cross in eight hours by only stopping at Grantham, York, Newcastle and Berwick'. This, be it remembered, was in 1853! It is important to note that from this stage all the initiative in East Coast speed-making came from the Great Northern. After its brief spell of prominence during the gauge trials, before the Great Northern ever existed, the line north of York sank into relative obscurity, and a placidity of operation that two races to the north did not entirely remove. But in the 1850s the Great Northern was prepared to lick the proverbial pants off anyone, and Sturrock declared that his great new engine 'could, and did run 100-mile lengths at the highest present speeds'. There are unfortunately no records of what the big 4-2-2 engine No 215 actually achieved. In many features of her design she showed strong resemblance to Gooch's eight-footers on the broad gauge Great Western, with its raised firebox and sandwich frames, even to the extent of having a hooded seat on the rear of the tender for the 'travelling porter'. Where Sturrock's design differed from Gooch's he got into trouble. He used a leading bogie. This also had a sandwich frame, but was made with such tight clearances from the main frames that damp weather caused the wood in both to swell and bind bogie and main frame up solid. The result was frequent derailments, accentuated by the fact that the driving wheels were flangeless. No one rose to Sturrock's challenge of an eight-hour run to Edinburgh, and although the bogie trouble was soon eradicated by the provision of more adequate clearances No 215 remained an odd engine, and had a short life of only seven years.

In the meantime events were moving in a different direction on the London & North Western Railway. McConnell's dashing outlook found no response in the Northern Division, based on Crewe – rather the reverse – and the situation began to cause some concern to the top management of the railway. Francis Trevithick, son of the mighty Richard, was the titular head of Crewe; but his administration was ineffective, and earned the scathing comment from Richard Moon: 'I look upon the labor for anyone taking Crewe to put it in order as herculean. No system could work with Trevithick's weak hand.' So, in 1857, the former North Eastern and Northern Divisions of the LNWR were amalgamated, and John Ramsbottom was put in charge of both, with headquarters at Crewe. At that time the Marquis of Chandos was chairman of the company; but already Richard Moon was a mighty power behind the throne and there is no doubt that he exercised an immense influence upon Ramsbottom from the moment he was appointed. Moon's precise and tidy mind looked towards the utmost efficiency in running the railway. He could countenance no expenditure unless he could see a handsome return for it. He saw no need for high speed; it involved increased wear and tear, and the express trains were well patronised. The standard of passenger train speed became stabilised for many years around the overall average of 42mph demanded by the Post Office contract for conveyance of the Irish Mail between Euston and Holyhead.

Ramsbottom had thus a very clear mandate so far as the provision of new motive power was concerned, and he produced locomotives that were in striking contrast to those of McConnell in the still-independent Southern Division of the LNWR. The only new design that need to be noticed in any detail is, curiously enough, the one that stood out in sharp distinction to the rest, namely the Lady of the Lake 7ft 6in single. Why Ramsbottom should have adopted outside cylinders and produced a locomotive that had a strong family likeness to a 2-2-2 that Patrick Stirling had built for the Glasgow & South Western two years earlier need not concern us here. The point is that the Lady of the Lake class came to play some part in the establishment of British railway speed records in later years, and their design is worthy of some study. Its basic characteristics can be highlighted by setting them alongside those of McConnell's latest and finest express engines for the Southern Division.

Division *Engine Class* *Designer*	*Northern* *Lady of the Lake* *J. Ramsbottom*	*Southern* *Extra-large Bloomer* *J. E. McConnell*
Type	2-2-2	2-2-2
Driving wheel diameter	7ft 6in	7ft 6in
Cylinders dia stroke	16in	18in
	24in	24in
Total heating surface	1,098sq ft	1,223sq ft
Grate area	14·9sq ft	26sq ft
Boiler pressure	120lb per sq in	150lb per sq in
Total weight, engine only	27 tons	34¾ tons

There was an equally astonishing contrast in their outward appearance, with the Lady in a plain dark green, with only a single black line to set off the surrounds of tender and footplate sides; and against this the brilliant pillar-box red of the Bloomer, set off by flashing brass and copper work wherever there was a fitting that gave the opportunity for high polish. One can readily imagine how the coldly practical and austere mind of Richard Moon would have viewed such positively flagrant diversities of practice, both in outward appearance and design; and there can be no doubt that he carefully compared the first cost of the two types of locomotives – not to the advantage of McConnell! The Extra-large Bloomers came out in 1861, however, at a time when Moon was temporarily bereft of power, and the reasons why only three of these splendid engines were built need no further explanation. Moon's return was also the cause of their falling so quickly into disfavour afterwards.

During the time of Lord Chandos's chairmanship Moon was chairman of the Stores Committee of the Board, and in 1858 he asked a number of awkward questions at the Board Table concerning the cost of certain activities at Wolverton. McConnell had many friends among the directors, and these men took up Moon's probing strongly, even making a personal issue of it. As a result Moon resigned his position as Chairman of the Stores Committee. But he remained on the Board, and the antagonism between him and McConnell deepened. But as long as Lord Chandos remained chairman all was well, and when the noble lord was succeeded in 1860 by Admiral Moorsom there was no change; it was in the following year that McConnell's super express locomotives began to appear from Wolverton. But Moorsom held office for only one year, and when he was succeeded by Moon, in 1861, McConnell realised his position would soon be untenable, and he resigned. This of course was the opportunity Moon had been hoping for. The Northern and Southern Divisions were amalgamated, and Ramsbottom was appointed Chief Mechanical Engineer of the entire railway. One of his earliest moves was to lower the boiler of the Bloomers from 150 to 120lb per sq in, clearly to reduce boiler maintenance costs; but it added to the friction that developed between Crewe and Wolverton, inevitably resulting from such an amalgamation.

Less than a year after the merger a political event of the first magnitude brought the locomotives of the LNWR very much into the public eye. It was the time of the American Civil War, when the rebel states of the south were anxious to obtain diplomatic recognition of their independence. Accordingly two prominent men sailed for Europe in the British merchant ship *Trent*; but the northern states got wind of this intention, and when 250 miles out from Havana the *Trent* was fired on by an American warship and stopped. The delegates were seized from under the protection of the British flag, and taken into custody. Feeling in England naturally ran very high and the government of the day delivered an ultimatum that, if its demands were refused, was tantamount to a declaration of war. The weeks that elapsed before the reply came through were a time of intense excitement, and the most careful preparations were made to convey the dispatch to London as quickly as possible. The route was to be the normal one of the inward-bound American mail via Queenstown, Cork, Dublin and Holyhead. From 2 January 1862 onwards Holyhead kept a first-class express engine ready for instant departure, but it was not until the evening of 6 January that the ss *Europa* reached Queenstown. The dispatch was conveyed to Cork by tender, and the GS&WR ran a special to Dublin. At 8.15am on 7 January the steamer was alongside the Admiralty pier at Holyhead. Light though the Lady of the Lake class engines were, they were not permitted to run on to the pier, and an old Allan single No 18 *Cerberus* worked the saloon, conveying the Queen's Messenger and a van round to the main station. There a Lady No 229 *Watt* was waiting to back on the front van, and then she was away to cover the 130½ miles to Stafford non-stop in 144 minutes, an average speed of 54·3mph.

Great importance had been set upon conveying the Queen's Messenger from Holyhead to Euston in five hours from the moment of the arrival of the steamer, an overall average of 52·7mph, and great stress was laid afterwards upon the value of Ramsbottom's newly installed water troughs, near Aber, which enabled a non-stop run of 130½ miles to be made. Actually the train did not stop in Stafford station, but at Trent Valley Junction half a mile to the south, where engine changing could be more expeditiously arranged. It was said at the time that the non-stop run from Holyhead was somewhat hampered by a strong cross-wind off the Irish Sea, and that in consequence the 59½ level miles from Bangor to Chester took as much as 68½ minutes, an average speed of only 52·3mph. But with so light a load one would have thought such a hindrance could have been overcome. At Stafford however things were organised to the last detail. On arrival *Watt* was uncoupled, and ran ahead on to the Birmingham line. Then waiting on the Trent Valley line was the Extra Large Bloomer No 372, and the whole operation of engine changing was so smartly done that the special was at rest for a mere 1½ minutes. Even so, if the overall time of five hours was to be maintained, only 141½ minutes remained in which to cover the remaining 133·1 miles to Euston. Furthermore fog was reported south of Kilsby Tunnel. There were no water troughs on the Southern Division at that time, and with further to go than the much vaunted Holyhead–Stafford non-stop the task set to No 372 might well have seemed a stiff one.

From the moment they were away from Trent Valley Junction, however, it was evident that the men on No 372 had no inhibitions! The first 49½ miles, to the junction with the Birmingham Line outside Rugby, took a mere 46½ minutes – a start to pass average of almost 64mph. Then the anticipated fog took its toll and the 50·9 miles from Rugby to Tring took 62 minutes. By Tring however they had struck clear weather once again, and by that time they had only 32 minutes left to complete the journey in five hours, with 31·7 miles to go. The engine was appropriately given her head, and the 29·3 miles from Tring to the north end of Primrose Hill Tunnel took only 26 minutes – an average of 67·7mph – and with time then comfortably in hand they coasted in to arrive at 1.13pm, two minutes inside schedule. The five hours were counted from the moment the steamer was alongside at Holyhead. The arrival in Euston had the elements of drama in it. Before the special had stopped, the Queen's Messenger, carrying the precious dispatch box, had jumped from the saloon, raced across to a waiting carriage and pair, and was driving through the gates on his way to Downing Street as engine No 372 came finally to rest!

So far as the locomotive performance was concerned, the honours, despite the publicity showered upon the water troughs, rested fairly and squarely upon the Southern Division. As compared to the average of 54·3mph from Holyhead to Trent Valley Junction, the Extra Large Bloomer had run the 133·1 miles to Euston in 139½ minutes, an average of 57·2mph, with no water troughs, and fully ten minutes lost by fog between Rugby and Tring. Had No 372 been able to continue in the same style throughout it is quite probable that a run of 126 or 127 minutes from Trent Valley Junction to Euston would have been made. This would have constituted a long distance high speed record for the period. Because of the prevailing 'atmosphere' on the LNWR towards anything that savoured of McConnell, the supreme significance of the performance of engine No 372 was discreetly passed over!

CHAPTER THREE

FORWARD TO THE 'EIGHTY-EIGHT'

IN ENGLISH history it has long been customary to distinguish between the two Scottish Jacobite rebellions of the eighteenth century as the 'fifteen' and the 'forty-five'; and it was a great Scottish Highland enthusiast, Norman Doran Macdonald, who chose to distinguish similarly between the two railway races to the north, in 1888 and 1895 – the 'eighty-eight' and the 'ninety-five'. But in this chronicle of mine a quarter of a century of very lean years have to be passed over before we reach the unprecedented excitement of a railway 'race' on the staid and comparatively well-ordered metals of Great Britain. There were nevertheless many cogent reasons why the early development that led to the fine achievements recorded in the two previous chapters came imperceptibly, but definitely, to a halt during the later 1860s. It was the realisation, not expressed in so many words, that railway speed had rather over-reached itself, and had pressed ahead of the technological advances that were essential to its regular and safe achievement. The period from 1865 to the very threshold of the 1888 'race' was certainly a black one for British railway history. Apart from the catastrophe of the first Tay Bridge, which was not concerned with speed, or operation of traffic, one can recall at least sixteen serious accidents in this period, the majority of which could be attributed to faulty rolling stock, a complete lack of interlocking of points and signals, absence of proper brakes, or deficient permanent way. Remarkably few could be marked up purely against lack of diligence or care on the part of the staff.

Time and again when some deficiency had caused derailment or parting of the couplings of a train, things were made infinitely worse by the complete absence of brake power on the section parted from the locomotive, which then proceeded to run wildly amok. This happened with a Great Northern express south of Hatfield; at Wigan in 1873 when the down Tourist express was wrecked; and at Wennington when part of a Midland train derailed by excessive speed over a junction ran unhindered to a frightful pile-up against the parapet of a bridge. It occurred most dramatically of all when the breaking of a crank axle on the locomotive of a Manchester, Sheffield & Lincolnshire express near Penistone caused a jerk that broke a van coupling immediately behind the tender; the subsequent derailment threw practically the whole train down a steep embankment. Then just imagine the extraordinary signalling muddle at Tamworth, in 1870, when lack of coordination between signalmen at each end of the station and lack of any interlocking led to the up night Irish Mail being routed at full speed into a pair of buffer-stops! I need not dwell upon the tragic and well-known circumstances of Staplehurst, Abergele, Abbots Ripton and Hexthorpe, nor to the practice of 'strengthening' over-crowded trains with old and dilapidated coaches, attached for ease of marshalling immediately behind the engine. The terrible consequences of this were emphasised in the Christmas Eve disaster near Shipton, Great Western Railway in 1874.

Managements were well enough aware of the hazards of operating; but there was a general reluctance to invest in improved equipment, particularly in block signalling and interlocking, continuous automatic brakes, and more substantial permanent way. It all cost money, and one particularly callous general manager stated publicly that he would rather pay the compensations for deaths and injuries in an occasional bad accident than go to the expense of fitting a brake he did not want! Those sixteen accidents were certainly spread around the major railways, with one each to the Great Western, South Eastern, Great Eastern, Midland, Somerset & Dorset, North Eastern, and Caledonian; two to the Great Northern, three to the Manchester, Sheffield & Lincolnshire and four to the London & North Western. One can well appreciate there was no desire to accelerate. The leisurely 40mph expresses of the North Western were well patronized and the train services of Great Britain as a whole were, in this period, so far advanced as to justify Professor Foxwell's carefully considered and world-wide summing up: 'England first, and the rest nowhere.' Enthusiasts north of the border may tilt at this use of the name England, seeing that Foxwell included in the adjective 'English' the Caledonian, North British, Glasgow & South Western, and Highland Railways! National susceptibilities apart, a connoisseur of railway train services the world over would have had no hesitation in placing Great Britain overwhelmingly first in the seventies of last century, unexciting though most of the running was compared with that of the period 1845–55.

How then did the leading north-going lines from London rouse themselves from this position of comfortable superiority to all the disturbance, anxieties and hazards of an undisguised race from London to Edinburgh in 1888? Its origin was purely commercial. During the summer service of 1887 and throughout the subsequent winter, the times of the morning Anglo-Scottish expresses leaving Kings Cross and Euston at 10am had been the traditional 9hr to Edinburgh by the East Coast Route and 10hr by the West Coast. The difference was that the Flying Scotsman conveyed only first and second class passengers whereas the Euston train conveyed all three classes. In November 1887 the East Coast companies suddenly announced that their Special Scotch Express, as the 10am from Kings Cross was then described, would convey third class passengers. At first it seemed that the West Coast partners were taking this important development with a 'So what?' type of attitude. After all, the 10am from Euston served Glasgow as well as Edinburgh. Before the winter of 1887–8 was out however it was evident that they were losing the cream of the third class business between London and Edinburgh, and much as the top management disliked the prospect acceleration was essential, solely on commercial grounds. I need not go through all the stages by which the schedules were gradually brought down to a level eight-hour by both competitors from 6 August 1888. We can pass on the splendid running made by both sides, and the new records for high-speed long-distance travelling that were achieved.

First of all, the North Western, in running the 158 miles from Euston to Crewe, made the longest non-stop run that had yet been scheduled anywhere in the world. Curiously enough however the booked average speed over this fine road was not so high as that scheduled over the 90 miles from Preston to Carlisle, over Shap. The North Western share of the eight-hour schedule was made up as follows:

Euston-Crewe: 158·1 miles, 180 minutes; 52·7 mph.
Crewe-Preston: 51 miles, 58 minutes; 52·8 mph.
Preston-Carlisle: 90·1 miles, 100 minutes; 54 mph.

No more than five minutes were allowed for engine changing at Crewe, but at Preston there was the traditional luncheon interval, and it is amusing to find that the passengers' digestions had to participate in the accelerations. Hitherto the luncheon stop had been 25 minutes, but from 6 August 1888 it was cut to 20. Carlisle was reached at 4.3pm, and after another engine-changing stop of 5min the Caledonian had the job of running the remaining 100·6 miles to Edinburgh over Beattock and Cobbinshaw summits in 112 minutes, an excellent average of 53·8mph. Thus the average overall speed, including all stops, was a fraction below 50mph, over 399·8 miles. The East Coast, with 7 miles less to go, made an average of 49·2mph, also with three intermediate stops.

The West Coast partners gave very special attention to comfortable riding. In their view speed alone would not bring back the declining third class business. The Edinburgh portion of the 10am from Euston was run separately throughout, ahead of the Glasgow portion, and consisted of four eight-wheeled non-bogie coaches of the latest West Coast Joint Stock type, with the Webb radial axles. Care was taken to keep them tightly coupled together, and the *ensemble* ran very smoothly with the action of a quadruple articulated unit. The load was 80 tons behind the tender. Even in relation to contemporary standards this was not a big train; but considering it was a highly competitive service, run at an unprecedentedly high average speed, it was enough. Furthermore, between Euston and Crewe the working was shared by two Ramsbottom 2-2-2 singles of the Lady of the Lake class. Whatever the top management at Euston may have thought of the whole affair there is no doubt Webb thoroughly entered into the spirit of racing. The Ladies were great favourites of his, and they managed the 52.7mph non-stop run from Euston to Crewe with ease. It is remarkable to find that on the great majority of the record runs to be described in the course of this book the load hauled, including the weight of the tender with the train, was roughly three times the weight of the engine itself. Between Euston and Crewe in 1888, it was rather higher. The Ladies weighed only 27 tons in working order, and their tenders another 25 tons. Thus the load behind the engine was 3·9 times the weight of the engine itself. The fastest run was on 13 August 1888, when 2-2-2 engine No 806 *Waverley* reached Crewe in 166 minutes, an average speed of 57·2mph. This was probably the fastest run ever made by an engine of this class, and it is important to appreciate that apart from having a cab, and the driving wheel splashers closed in, the engine was in its original Ramsbottom condition, *before* the virtual renewal of the whole class by Webb in 1895, with larger boilers and higher boiler pressure.

Between Crewe and Carlisle the Precedent class 2-4-0s were used, and they too had no difficulty in keeping time. The fastest run made was by engine No 275 *Vulcan* on 7 August, when ten minutes were gained on schedule between

Preston and Carlisle, and a start-to-stop average speed of 60mph achieved. In view of the mountainous nature of the route this needs special mention, bearing in mind once again that the engine was hauling 3·24 times its own weight. The following is a log, with times taken to the nearest half-minute:

Distance miles		*Time minutes*	*Average Speed mph*
0·0	PRESTON	0	—
21·0	LANCASTER	21	60·0
27·3	CARNFORTH	26½	68·8
34·6	Milnthorpe	33	67·4
40·1	Oxenholme	39	55·0
47·2	Grayrigg	48	47·3
53·2	Tebay	53½	65·5
60·7	Shap station	63½	45·0
72·2	PENRITH	73	72·0
79·3	Calthwaite	80	61·0
85·2	Wreay	85	70·8
90·1	CARLISLE	90	

On this run the time of passing Shap Summit was not taken; but assuming it took about 2½ minutes to cover the 2 miles from that point to Shap station the time would have been about 61 minutes from Preston, indicating a remarkable uphill time of 34½ minutes for the 31·4 miles from Carnforth to Summit. Such an average speed as 54½mph over a section with a vertical rise of 885ft was quite outstanding for the period, seeing that the average inclination throughout this 31½ miles is about 1 in 185. There was also some quite uninhibited fast running downhill to yield *average* speeds of over 70mph from Shap station down to Penrith, and again from Calthwaite to Wreay. This run was certainly a foretaste of still finer things to come from the little 33-ton Precedent 2-4-0s.

On the Caledonian, the haulage of the Edinburgh flyer was entrusted to only one engine throughout the racing period, and that a single-wheeler, of all types, for the route in question. But of course, engine No 123 was no ordinary single-wheeler; she was by far the largest and heaviest locomotive used by the West Coast companies during the race, and her nominal tractive effort of 12,700lb put very much in the shade the 10,830lb of a North Western Precedent, and still more so the 6,900lb of a Lady of the Lake. Furthermore the Caledonian No 123 weighed 43 tons without her tender. These statistics are not intended to denigrate in any way the magnificent and consistent performance of this famous engine, but to put her work into proper perspective beside that of her contemporaries. So far as gradients were concerned she had by far the hardest task of any engine on either side in the whole race, having not only to surmount the 1,014ft altitude of Beattock summit, but from the slow negotiation of the junctions at Carstairs to climb again to Cobbinshaw, 880ft above sea level. On the apparent difficult timing of 112 minutes for the 100·6 miles, engine No 123 made twenty-three runs. On four occasions the time was 110 minutes; on another six it was 109; and on seven days it was 108. On the remaining six days it varied from 107 down to a truly brilliant 102½ minutes on Thursday 9 August.

Dugald Drummond was taking as keen an interest in the day-to-day progress of the race as Webb was doing at Crewe, and the record run of 9 August is fortunately most fully documented. Drummond issued to *The Engineer* a diagram showing the speed run over every mile of the journey, and from this the accompanying log has been prepared, showing the performance over the more significant stretches of line. One would naturally expect a brisk start from Carlisle, slightly downhill to the crossing of the Solway Firth near Gretna; but then the next 41·1 miles to Beattock Summit, involving a vertical rise of almost 1,000ft, took only 43min 26sec, an average speed of 56·9mph. The average inclination of 1 in 217 is a little easier than the North Western of 1 in

185 from Carnforth up to Shap Summit, and the locomotive effort involved would be much the same, though sustained for a longer period on the Caledonian.

9 August 1888

Distance miles		*Time min sec*	*Average Speed mph*
0·0	CARLISLE	0 00	—
8·6	Gretna Junction	9 38	53·5
39·7	BEATTOCK	39 13	63·1
49·7	*Summit*	53 04	43·3
72·0	*Milepost 72*	73 28	65·5
73·2	*Strawfrank Junction**	74 44	57·2
74·8	Carnwath	77 16	37·9
82·2	Cobbinshaw	85 13	55·8
100·0	*Milepost 100*	101 28	65·7
100·6	EDINBURGH	102 33	

* Severe speed restriction

Downhill the maximum speed did not exceed 74mph at any point, and undoubtedly the finest achievement was that of the uphill running between Gretna and Beattock Summit. The last 5·7 miles of the Beattock bank, on a gradient averaging around 1 in 75, were covered in 8min 46sec at an average of 39·1mph. The absolute minimum was 36½mph.

Thus the best West Coast performances in the 'eighty-eight' can be summarised as on page 50.

There was not the same consistency of running on the North Western, nor of course was there the need. The two runs tabulated above involved substantial gains on the schedule times laid down; but where it is a question of records they must necessarily take priority over the more ordinary timekeeping runs.

On the East Coast Route Patrick Stirling himself contributed to *The Engineer* a most comprehensive summary

Railway	*Engine*	*Section*	*Distance miles*	*Time min*	*Av Speed mph*
LNWR	*Waverley*	Euston–Crewe	158·1	166	57·2
LNWR	*Vulcan*	Preston–Carlisle	90·1	90	60·0
Caledonian	123	Carlisle–Edinburgh	100·6	102½	58·8

of the running between Kings Cross and York throughout the month of August 1888. Between Kings Cross and Grantham the remarkable feature of the racing period was the number of different engines that were employed. On the twenty-seven days included in Stirling's own summary ten different engines were used, three of which were 7ft 6in 2-2-2s, and the remainder eight-foot bogie 4-2-2s. The fastest run from Kings Cross to Grantham took place on 25 August when a 2-2-2 No 233 covered the 105·5 miles in 105 minutes at an average speed of 60·3mph. Curiously enough, of the six runs made in 110 minutes or less four were made by the 2-2-2 engines. The fastest run by a bogie eight-footer was in 109 minutes by No 22 on 29 August. The 4-2-2 engines were wonderfully consistent in their performance, and it is a great tribute to the standards of maintenance on the Great Northern that it did not seem to matter which of them was put on. For the record, the individual 2-2-2s employed were Nos 233, 234 and 237, and the bogie eight-footers were Nos 7, 22, 48, 69, 98, 671 and 776.

Between Grantham and York only four engines, all bogie eight-footers, were used during the racing period, namely Nos 3, 95, 775 and 777. The overall times for this stretch of 82·7 miles varied only between the narrow limits of 88 and 92 minutes, but on 25 August Stirling's report claims that delays caused a loss of 9 minutes, and that the net time was 81 minutes. One can hardly claim records on the basis of an estimated net time without knowing the precise nature of the delays experienced, and thus the net average of 61·2mph from Grantham to York must remain unconfirmed. The fastest Great Northern start-to-stop run in the 1888 race was the 60.3mph average from Kings Cross to Grantham, by the 2-2-2 engine No 233 on 25 August. Until 20 August the load was usually one of eight six-wheeled coaches weighing about 120 tons tare. For the fast culmination of the race one coach less was taken, making a tare load of about 105 tons behind the tender. In contrast to the exceptionally smooth riding of the West Coast eight-wheelers the ECJS stock gave a hard, jogging ride, though not perhaps justifying the famous crack of E. L. Ahrons who said there were times when he suspected they had octagonal wheels!

The Great Northern authorities, despite the enterprise of their timetabling on all express routes, strongly deprecated any fast downhill running. Stirling strove to work even the fastest trains without much exceeding 70mph. The permanent way was not in good condition, and the riding of both locomotives and coaches could be unpleasant at times. The faster end-to-end times were made by harder running uphill. Although at the time of the 'eighty-eight' the Great Northern was probably the fastest line in the world so far as its booked express services were concerned, it contributed little to the record of speed achievement in the race, other than a very striking demonstration of the steady reliability of its locomotives to maintain average speeds of 55 to 58mph. In this respect, of course, the Great Northern was well in advance of its contemporaries. All the other companies concerned in the 'eighty-eight' used specially selected engines and kept them continuously on the job. On the Great Northern, particularly between Kings Cross and Grantham, it did not seem to matter what engine was put on, 2-2-2 and 4-2-2 alike; they all did the job with consistent excellence.

Apart from the North Western use of the Lady of the Lake 2-2-2s, on the Euston–Crewe non-stop run the big surprise of the 'eighty-eight' was the way in which the North

Eastern rose to the occasion. For many years that company had been regarded as a particularly laggard partner in the East Coast alliance. The North Eastern had such a comfortable monopoly in its own area, and derived such a princely revenue from its large short-haul freight and mineral traffic, that its management did not seem to worry unduly about the speed of passenger train services, including its participation in the Anglo-Scottish traffic by the East Coast Route. It was generally thought that when competition did arise, to the intensity generated in the 'eighty-eight', the North Eastern would be content to jog along as of old and leave the business of acceleration to the Great Northern.

On the other hand a new drive and purpose had come into the locomotive department since the easy-going days of Edward Fletcher, and the stormy era of Alexander McDonnell. Thomas Worsdell was in the chair at Gateshead, and there was a desire on all hands to show off the merits of the new two-cylinder compound engines, arranged on the Worsdell-Von Borries system. Between York and Newcastle however the supremely elegant 2-4-0s of the so-called Tennant class were used on the fastest trains. Few locomotive designs can, at their very first appearance, have been greeted with greater enthusiasm by the footplate men. Built in emergency, after the débâcle of the McDonnell régime, they were a larger and more powerful version of all that had been most popular on the North Eastern in the days of Edward Fletcher. They were introduced in 1885, and by the time of the 'race' they were universal favourites on the line. Although of the 2-4-0 wheel arrangement they were considerably larger and heavier than the North Western Precedents, with 18in by 24in cylinders, a boiler pressure of 160lb per sq in and a total weight of 42 tons, against the 33 tons of the LNWR contemporaries. With 7ft diameter coupled wheels also they were real flyers.

During the fastest phase of the 'eighty-eight' the Tennants were running the 80·6 miles from York to Newcastle in 80 to 82 minutes, day after day. At that time also the approach to Newcastle Central was more roundabout than from 1906 onwards. There was then only one railway bridge over the Tyne in the city area, the High Level; and trains from the south had to run past Gateshead works and running sheds, and make a slow approach over the sharp curves at Gateshead High Street and over the famous crossing at the east end of Newcastle Central station. It is unfortunate that no intermediate details have been preserved of the occasion on which engine No 1475 ran through from York to Newcastle in 78 minutes, for this was actually one minute faster than the fastest time made in the 'ninety-five'. But this average speed of 62mph is a tremendous feather in the cap of the Tennant locomotives, and although not fully authenticated to the extent of a detailed log it was probably the fastest start-to-stop run made during the 'eighty-eight'.

Details are available of a fast run made by the same engine on the last day of the race, with the usual load of seven six-wheeled coaches having a tare weight of 105 tons. The Tennants had the reputation of being leisurely starters, and in taking 24½ minutes to cover the initial 22·2 miles from York to Thirsk No 1475 was certainly running true to form. By then, however, she was going in fine style, and Darlington 44·1 miles was passed in 44¾ minutes at 70mph. Then, unfortunately, there was a dead stand for signals for 1¾ minutes outside Ferryhill, so that it took 69 minutes to pass Durham, 66·0 miles. Some fast running was made down the bank from Chester-le-Street, with four consecutive miles covered at average speeds of 75¾, 75¾, 76½ and 76½mph, and Newcastle was reached in 83½ minutes, despite the stop, and a further check near Chester-le-Street. The net time is estimated at approximately 80 minutes, an average of 60.5mph from York.

North of Newcastle the North Eastern relied mainly upon the new Worsdell-Von Borries compound 4-4-0s of the F class, but unfortunately the evidence of actual running times does not seem to be reliable enough for any definite records to be claimed. For example, one of the compounds was stated to have run the 124·4 miles from Newcastle to Edinburgh in 125 minutes; but while the time was not subsequently disproved it was revealed that the train had been double-headed. On the last day of the race a 4-4-0 compound, No 117, made a fast run with the normal load of 105 tons; but while some authorities claim that the overall time was 126 minutes, others give nothing faster than 130. In such circumstances no definite performance can be established, other than the fact that the Worsdell-Von Borries compounds were fast and free-running locomotives. T. W. Worsdell, as an ex-Crewe man, would undoubtedly have been taking the closest interest in the prowess of the famous Webb compounds, and as a shrewd onlooker would have been aware of certain factors that made them relatively sluggish. No such criticism could be levelled against his own compound locomotives, and it is a pity that no more detailed records exist of the work of the F class between Newcastle and Edinburgh, during the 'eighty-eight'.

The race left us with three definite records of start-to-stop average speeds of 60mph and over, made by the North Western Precedent from Preston to Carlisle, by the Stirling 2-2-2 No 233 from Kings Cross to Grantham, and by the North Eastern Tennant from York to Newcastle – speeds of 60, 60·3 and 62mph respectively. It is a pity, from the viewpoint of outright speeding, that the Worsdell 7ft 7in 4-2-2s of the J class did not come out until the following year, for they were unquestionably the fastest engines yet to run on British metals. These engines were also introduced as compounds, and fortunately some very detailed records of their performance are available, as a result of indicator trials carried out with engine No 1518. For single-wheelers, particularly with driving wheels as large as 7ft 7in diameter, they were very powerful engines. The proportions of the high and low pressure cylinders had been most successfully arranged so as to distribute the work, with remarkable equality between the two, and the exhaust system permitted of a very free flow of steam. Some astonishing results were obtained on trials between Newcastle and Berwick.

The engine was not only taken up to 75mph but was worked hard at that speed to develop no less than 1,041 indicated horsepower. As if this were not enough the cut-offs in both cylinders were further increased, and a maximum speed of no less than 86mph and an outstanding output of 1,069 indicated horsepower obtained. All this was done under the severely critical eye of Walter M. Smith, who was the rising power behind the throne at Gateshead. In the same group of trials, but under lighter steaming conditions, the sister engine No 1517 reached a maximum speed of 90mph when hauling a load of eighteen six-wheeled coaches. In passing, one just wonders how some of those coaches were riding, at 90mph! The North Eastern had not got a dynamometer car at that time, and the drawbar horsepower was not recorded. On certain other occasions they borrowed Webb's little six-wheeled dynamometer car from Crewe. There was however no doubt that the J class 4-2-2s could pull as well as run, for No 1517 is recorded as having worked a train of 270 tons (32 carriages) from Newcastle to Berwick, 66·9 miles, in 78 minutes.

In view of such splendid results one can indeed ask why these engines were so soon converted into two-cylinder simples, without in any way diminishing their speed-worthiness. One of the features in design that contributed to the sluggishness of the Webb compounds on the LNWR was the restriction in size of the low pressure cylinders in relation to the volume of the high pressure. Gateshead made no such mistake with the J class, and in conjunction with a high pressure cylinder 20in diameter, the low pressure was made no less than 28in diameter. The relative proportions were exactly right, as W. M. Smith's indicator tests on engine No 1518 proved beyond any doubt. But that huge low pressure cylinder was an embarrassment in another respect. Both cylinders were placed high up, and inclined, and the low pressure was so near to the underside of the boiler that there was no room for the steam chests between the frames. Both the high pressure and low pressure steam chests were therefore placed outside the frames, and the valves were worked by rocking levers. The combination of these outside steam chests, and the complications of the rocking shaft mechanism from the inside Joy's gear, led to troubles in operation, and hastened the decision to rebuild them as two-cylinder simples, with 19in by 24in cylinders, and Smith's patent piston valves. As such they remained very speedy engines.

Before we leave the 'eighty-eight' and with it the 1881–90 decade, mention should be made of the general maximum of railway speeds then attained on the railways of Great Britain. Apart from the all-out broad gauge trials by Brunel and Gooch on the Dauntsey incline, when 78mph was attained by several of the 8ft 4-2-2 engines, the general maximum was around 75mph. In 1884 indeed, Rous-Marten, reporting to the New Zealand Government, gave his opinion that the ordinary limit of attainable velocity was somewhere about 75mph. This is certainly born out by the fastest running made by all the competing locomotives in the 'eighty-eight'. Until the advent of the Worsdell J class 4-2-2 compounds the maximum speed that can be claimed as fully authenticated in Great Britain was recorded by E. L. Ahrons in 1887 from the footplate of a broad gauge 8ft 4-2-2 down the Wellington bank. The engine was hauling four bogie coaches, and at Ahrons's instigation the engine was driven to attain the utmost possible speed. The result was a maximum of 81·8mph – a mile in exactly 44 seconds; but Ahrons then regarded this as quite exceptional.

CHAPTER FOUR

DECADE OF THE 'NINETY-FIVE'

THE LAST ten years of the nineteenth century witnessed some astonishing advances in the speed of railway travel. For more than forty years maximum speeds had remained so constant at around 75mph as to cause so acute an observer as Charles Rous-Marten to give his considered opinion that such a maximum represented the ultimate with steam locomotives. And then steadily but quite definitely speeds began to rise. I have referred at some length to the exceptional performance of the North Eastern two-cylinder compound 4-2-2s. They, it is true, were new engines, of what was then a very advanced design. But older engines were showing greater capacity for high speed, and this phenomenon was discussed at some length among the few, but most erudite, railway enthusiasts of the day. E. L. Ahrons, as a trained and widely experienced mechanical engineer, has advanced the most likely explanation. Not only were steel rails coming into general use, together with steel tyres, but much harder steels were being introduced. Running over such rails would have much less deflection than hitherto, and the resistance to motion would be less. Improvements were also being made in the quality of the road-bed, with better ballasting and better drainage; these latter had been in progress over a longer period, and there can be little doubt that it was the quality of the rails themselves and of locomotive wheel tyres that made the greatest contribution.

Before what a reluctant participant once referred to as the 'disturbance' of 1895 broke upon the East and West Coast routes from London to Scotland other railways had begun to show their form in high speed running. On 11 July 1891, an Adams 7ft outside cylinder 4-4-0 of the London & South Western Railway reached and sustained a maximum speed of 81mph descending from Honiton tunnel to Seaton Junction, and in the course of a series of trials with this same engine on both the West of England and Bournemouth routes speeds up to 78mph were attained. Normal schedules on the South Western did not call for such high speeds; but the Adams seven-footer attained its maximum of 81mph under relatively easy steam, working in 17 per cent cut off though admittedly on a steeply falling gradient. What the London, Chatham & Dover could do was shown in startling fashion five years later; but that was after the second great railway race had eventuated. It was on the Midland that evidence of an upward move beyond the previous 75mph 'ceiling' was apparent, even before the race. Midland claims for an out-and-out record however, did not come until a few years later. So the railways of Britain entered the 'nineties' with the North Eastern holding the record for maximum speed, at 90mph, while for a start-to-stop run the Great Western records of 1846 and 1848, of 67mph from Paddington to Didcot, still remained unbeaten.

The build-up towards the race of 'ninety-five' began in mid-July when the West Coast companies suddenly announced on the morning of Monday 15 that on the very next morning the 8pm Tourist express from Euston would reach Aberdeen at 7am instead of the 7.40am worked during the preceding six weeks. From the very start of this accelerated working however some highly unorthodox operating methods were employed. As most of the running took place in the dead of night it was quite a long time before the East Coast came to realise what was going on, and that although schedule times were laid down, on each day and every night the West Coast were running the racing portion of the 8pm from Euston as fast as they could. There was no question of waiting for time at intermediate stations; as soon as engines were changed and the train was ready it was signalled away.

This procedure was followed with equal vigour and enthusiasm at Crewe, Carlisle, Stirling and Perth, and although the advertised time of arrival continued to be 7am right down to 18 August the actual arrivals in Aberdeen between 29 July and 18 August varied between 6.23am at the very latest and an astonishing 5.59am – 61 minutes early!

On this last occasion the overall average speed from London to Aberdeen was 54mph. From 29 July the East Coast booked their train in at 6.25am but between that date and 18 August they were on time or early on only six occasions out of eighteen, and only once in this same period did they arrive in Aberdeen ahead of the West Coast, despite the fact that they had sixteen miles less to run. The very fastest East Coast run up to that time gave an arrival of 6.17am – 617 minutes for the journey of 524 miles, and an overall average speed of 51mph. Even at this stage however affairs were working up to a pitch of great excitement, because of the convergence of the rival routes at Kinnaber Junction, three miles to the north of Montrose. Whichever train was first offered, the East Coast from Montrose or the West Coast from Dubton Junction, got the road, and led the way for the remaining 38 miles to Aberdeen. By that time both routes were fully signalled and interlocked throughout, so that the old time hazards of train operation had fortunately been eliminated. From the locomotive and train working points of view both routes were already surpassing themselves. Until 19 August the North Western was using Precedents exclusively, both north and south of Crewe. On five occasions, when the load was heavier than usual, Lady of the Lake class 2-2-2s were used as pilots. These were the renewed engines, with larger boilers, and a working pressure of 150lb per sq in; a more powerful proposition altogether than the *Marmion* and *Waverley* that did so gallantly in the 'eighty-eight'.

On the Caledonian, with the exception of two days, there were only two drivers concerned between Carlisle and Perth, from the acceleration of 15 July to the end of the race, each with his own engine. These were the splendid Drummond 6ft 6in 4-4-0s, and from the very outset Driver Crooks with engine No 90 and driver T. Robinson with engine No 78 made some wonderful running. On his very first run Robinson covered the 150 miles from Carlisle to Perth in 167 minutes, inclusive of a stop at Stirling. This was considerably better than the best North Western standards for the month of July, when the time for the 158 miles from Euston to Crewe was gradually brought down from 180 to 170 minutes, and the 141 miles from Crewe to Carlisle were taking between 158 and 173 minutes. Seeing that the Caledonian had to surmount Beattock summit, and then after stopping at Stirling to climb again up to Gleneagles, their overall average of 54mph from Carlisle to Stirling was outstanding. It is true that the Drummond 4-4-0 was a considerably more powerful engine than a North Western Precedent but even so their drivers had entered upon the critical stage of the competition in tremendous form.

The East Coast acceleration, from 29 July, did not involve running equal to the best that had been achieved in the 'eighty-eight'. But that side had not yet entered into the spirit of real racing. The load hauled was 180 tons from Kings Cross and 195 tons from York, and over one section of the line at any rate time was actually lost. The principal centre of interest in the East Coast Route at this stage in the competition was the performance of the North British locomotives and their crews. Until 29 July these were more or less an unknown quantity. North British men had not been involved at all in the 'eighty-eight', because the Flying Scotsman was hauled non-stop from Newcastle to Edinburgh by the North Eastern.

Now, in the 'ninety-five', the North British had a particularly vital part to play. On all other sections of line, while there were occasional stations and junctions where a marked reduction of speed was required, such as Preston and Forfar on the West Coast Route, and Peterborough, Selby and Berwick on the East Coast, elsewhere it was good open road where drivers could settle down to long sustained spells of fast running. North of Edinburgh on the East Coast Route a road of exceptional difficulty faced the racing drivers. As this came to be the scene of some of the most extraordinary running ever made in Great Britain more than a passing reference is needed to the physical characteristics of the route.

To begin with it is most important to appreciate that the section between Edinburgh and Dundee was not in the first place planned as a single entity. It did not, in fact, reach its present form until 1890, when the Forth Bridge was opened. Until then it had been a series of bits and pieces built to serve the local needs of Fife, and although a direct line crossing the Firths of Forth and Tay had for many years been envisaged the lines that were eventually connected up to form that route had not been laid out for fast running. While Fife is not a mountainous country it is hilly, and its coastline much indented. One feels however that if its great importance had been foreseen the chain of railways linking up between the Forth and the Tay might have been engineered rather differently. As it was, prime costs seem to have been a major consideration. There are many awkward curves that could surely have been avoided, and with more enterprise in the engineering – admittedly at greater expense – the gradients could have been lessened.

In contrast also to the magnificent layouts built by the master-hands of the railway engineering profession, as evidenced on the Caledonian main line by Joseph Locke, some of the work in Fife was not very clever in its execution. There was the extraordinary case of Kinghorn Tunnel. I had never realised what this was like at all till I rode through for the first time on the footplate, and was warned to hang on tight.

Admiration knows no bounds when reading of the skilful surveying and construction of the great Alpine tunnels, bored simultaneously from both ends on courses set by precision instrumentation; and then far below some great mountain, four or five miles in from either end the two parties would meet, with a discrepancy of perhaps no more than a single inch in the vertical and lateral alignment. At Kinghorn, however, with a tunnel less than half a mile long, the parties missed by the whole width of the tunnel! The only way to correct such a ghastly error was to put in a reverse curve. And so it remains today, with a 25mph speed restriction in the midst of what should have been an entirely straight piece of railway. In steam days certain liberties used to be taken with that speed restriction, and to be ready for the S-bend in the blackness of the tunnel one had indeed to hang on!

I have dwelt rather upon Kinghorn Tunnel, not so much as an error in surveying, but as one of the many hazards in express train running over this route. The permanent speed restrictions are many, and some of the worst come most inconveniently at the foot of the steep gradients. Inverkeithing is a particularly bad location, at the foot of the very severe 1 in 70 bank before the longer incline that leads northward to Dalgetty summit. A steeply graded switchback route is no handicap in itself to the maintenance of a high average speed. There is the classic case of the Salisbury–Exeter main line of the London & South Western, engineered by Joseph Locke, over which the alignment is straight enough to permit of the highest speeds to be reached downhill in order to charge the steep ascents that invariably follow. But that is just what one cannot do between Edinburgh and Dundee. In addition to Inverkeithing there are slacks at Burntisland, Ladybank Junction, Cupar, Leuchars Junction, and over the sharp curve entering upon the Tay Bridge from the south. Burntisland is a bad one, shortly followed by Kinghorn Tunnel. The others are not so severe, but cumulatively they form a continuing source of hindrance. In recent years a very serious colliery subsidence has developed at Thornton Junction; but there was little in the way of speed reduction required at this point at the time of the 'ninety-five'.

From what I have written so far it will be appreciated that

with strict observance of all the speed restrictions it could be a slow business over that 59¼ miles from Edinburgh to Dundee. Even at the height of the 'ordinary' competition with the Caledonian for the Edinburgh–Aberdeen traffic that began in 1906 and lasted for a few years the time scheduled was as much as 80 minutes for this 59¼ miles, non-stop, and this was the fastest time being worked in the early days of grouping, in the 1920s. It is true that relatively heavy trains were then being worked, but with the capable and powerful Reid superheated Atlantics. As if the Edinburgh–Dundee section were not sufficient of a handicap, the line north of Dundee included a stretch of single line, from Arbroath, through Montrose to the junction with the Caledonian Railway at Kinnaber. This section also includes some very bad gradients. The single-line tokens had to be exchanged by hand, and the passing places were also in awkward locations in respect of subsequent gradients, particularly at Arbroath and Montrose. So, taking everything into consideration, the way the North British were going to shape up to the atmosphere of racing over such a route was one very big question. From 29 July the scheduled times laid down were 73 minutes for the Edinburgh–Dundee stage; 22 minutes, start to stop, for the 17 level miles on to Arbroath, and then 69 minutes for the final 54·2 miles to the Aberdeen ticket platform.

The respective average speeds over the three successive North British sections were thus 48·7, 46·3 and 47·1mph, and on paper they looked somewhat lethargic compared to the Great Northern averages of 54·5mph from Kings Cross to Grantham and 56·3mph from Grantham to York. It is true that the Dundee–Arbroath booking was not very brilliant, and traditional working on that fine level stretch was to let the East Coast Route down on at least one vital occasion in the following weeks; but the other two schedules were, in relation to the nature of the route, exceptionally severe. There was however another factor that undoubtedly helped the North British, and that was the traditional rivalry with the Caledonian. At this stage in time it is perhaps difficult to appreciate the intense feeling that existed between some of the old railway companies, particularly in Scotland. This was not merely a commercial rivalry between managements; it extended right down to the humblest workmen on either side. To the North British express enginemen the race gave them a heaven-sent opportunity to score points off the Caledonian. The initial timing of 73 minutes from Edinburgh to Dundee, fast though it was by later standards, was not unduly venturesome. It undoubtedly envisaged very rapid recoveries from the various slacks, with a powerful engine and a light train, and the gaining of time, as compared to later standards, where it would otherwise have been impracticable. They certainly had some excellent engines in the Holmes 6ft 6in 4-4-0s.

Had the North British stuck to the rules so far as speed restrictions were concerned the East Coast route would not have had any hope of running on equality with their rivals, even though the route from London to Aberdeen was some 16 miles shorter. With the North Eastern and the Caledonian stepping up their average speeds to over 55mph over every stage of the route, those North British averages of 46 to 48mph would have constituted a crippling handicap for which even the fastest efforts of the Great Northern and North Eastern would not have provided compensation. But from the end of July 1895 it was clear that the North British drivers were prepared to take the curves and difficult junctions at considerably higher speeds than those prescribed by the civil engineer. An experienced driver can tell when the riding of a locomotive is becoming unsafe, and little by little the North British men hotted up the pace. Day to day experience showed them that they could venture faster, and venture they certainly did!

Here I am concerned solely with speed records, but in passing I must give a momentary thought to how those ECJS six-wheeled coaches were riding. On many occasions when speed records were being broken the locomotives were riding perfectly, while the passengers were being treated to experiences not far short of terrifying!

The East Coast acceleration of 29 July was completely abortive in its attempt to stem the tide of West Coast speeding. Aberdeen was reached two minutes inside the new schedule of 10 hours 25 minutes, but after this had been done at the expense of considerable effort all round it was found that the West Coast had already been there 17 minutes. No further acceleration was attempted during the busiest part of the summer tourist traffic, culminating in the extreme pressure just prior to the opening of the grouse-shooting season on 12 August. But from 19 August the East Coast made an all-out attempt to secure a decision and finally establish the superiority that their shorter route would seem to imply. From that time onwards it was an undisguised race. Both sides had timetables laid down, but both were intending to go through as fast as they could, leaving intermediate stations as soon as they were ready, and not waiting for booked time. There was a misunderstanding over this at Edinburgh on the first day of the final week, and the train was held unnecessarily for eight minutes. This was not enough to lose the race, for the West Coast 'won' by 16 minutes on that particular occasion; but it was a delay to be avoided in future, particularly as the West Coast had clearly not yet reached their limit. The train that left Euston on the evening of 19 August had indeed made the astonishing overall average speed of 58·4mph over the 540 miles to Aberdeen – a feat that could well have seemed no more than a fairy tale only a month earlier.

The mounting excitement of the next three days has been recalled on many occasions. Here I am concerned principally with statistics, and the whole sheaf of new records that were made.

First of all there were the long-distance average speeds. On the night of 20/21 August, when the West Coast won the race to Kinnaber by a mere four minutes, the bare details were:

LONDON TO KINNABER

		East Coast	*West Coast*
Distance from London	miles	485·7	501·7
Total time	min	506	502
Average speed	mph	57·8	59·9
Total running time	min	493	489
Average running speed	mph	59·2	61·5

That night the North British had brought the Edinburgh–Dundee time down to an absolutely incredible 60½ minutes – a feat that would take some believing by anyone thoroughly familiar with running conditions over that section of line. This and the even faster run on the succeeding night are analysed later.

On the night of 21/22 August both sides ran a magnificently even race, and the advantage in distance gave victory to the East Coast. The overall results into Aberdeen passenger station were:

East Coast	523·5 miles	520 min	60·3 mph
West Coast	539·5 miles	534 min	60·5 mph

Having achieved this the East Coast quit the field, and left the West Coast to make an astonishing final record on the night of 22/23 August, when they reached Aberdeen at 4.32am with the overall time of 512 minutes showing an average speed of 63·2mph. No such run had ever previously been made anywhere in the world, by any form of transport, and despite all recent developments in railway motive power it still remains the London–Aberdeen land record.

Purely as regards start-to-stop average speeds the four fastest runs were:

Railway	*Engine No*	*Engine Class*	*Load tons*	*Section*	*Distance miles*	*Time min*	*Av Speed mph*
GNR	775	Stirling 4-2-2	101	Grantham–York	82·7	76	65·3
NER	1620	M class 4-4-0	101	Newcastle–Edinburgh	124·4	113	66·1
Caledonian	17	Lambie 4-4-0	72½	Perth–Aberdeen*	89·7	80½	66·8
LNWR	790	Precedent 2-4-0	72½	Crewe–Carlisle	141·0	126	67·2

* Ticket platform

It is remarkable that the fastest run of all was made over the most difficult route, but for resolute and fearless enginemanship the North Eastern run from Newcastle to Edinburgh must be bracketed nearly equal to it, albeit made by a much larger and potentially more powerful engine. In order to get a comparison between the running on the comparatively graded sections of line one may set the 73·4 miles from Minshull Vernon to Carnforth against the 75·0 miles from Longhirst to Dunbar. Each includes one very slack portion – at Preston on the LNWR and at Berwick on the North Eastern. This method of analysis gives the following result.

Route	*Distance miles*	*Time min*	*Av Speed mph*
West Coast	73·4	64½	68·3
East Coast	75·0	66¾	67·3

This shows very little in it. But then, whereas the North Eastern engine continued to run fast over the more or less level gradients of the Lothian Coast, the amazing little

North Western Precedent No 790 *Hardwicke* had to climb Shap. By the time she had topped the 915ft altitude of Shap Summit she had made the 'flying' average, over 104·8 miles from Minshull Vernon, of 66·5mph! The corresponding average of the North Eastern No 1620 over the 101·2 miles from Longhirst to Portobello was 68·4mph. As can be inferred from this the latter engine travelled very fast along the Lothian Coast covering the 26·2 miles from Dunbar to Portobello in exactly 22 minutes, at an average of 71·5mph. *Hardwicke* came down from Shap like a thunderbolt covering the 24·5 miles from Shap station to Wreay in 18¾ minutes at an *average* of 78·5mph, and her flying average over the 131·3 miles from Minshull Vernon to Wreay was 68·3mph. This magnificent feat easily carried off the British record for such a distance.

Perhaps even more astonishing was the fact that *Hardwicke*, having averaged 68·3mph over the more level part of the route from Minshull Vernon to Carnforth, took the 58 miles of mountain road from Carnforth up to Shap Summit and down to Wreay at precisely the same average. Before analysing the more technical aspects of *Hardwicke*'s run, it is interesting to examine some of the other flying averages:

Railway	*Engine*	*Section*	*Distance miles*	*Time min*	*Speed mph*
GNR	4-2-2 No 668	Wood Green–Stoke Box	95·1	88¾	64·2
GNR	4-2-2 No 775	Barkston–Naburn	74·3	65¾	67·7
LNWR	1309 *Adriatic*	Watford–Stafford	116·1	107	65·0
Caledonian	4-4-0 No 90	Gretna–Forgandeny	138·3	132¼	62·8
Caledonian	4-4-0 No 17	Stanley Junc Ferryhill	82·0	71	69·3

The Stirling 8-footer No 775 had the advantage on the 10 mile descent to the Trent valley, from Barkston, but the handicap of the slack through Selby. The Caledonian 4-4-0 No 17 put up a remarkable show, though except for a moderate slack through Forfar she had a good road throughout. For sheer skill in enginemanship however the work of the crew of the Caledonian engine No 90 was perhaps the finest achievement of the whole race. For the first time in history they were attempting a non-stop run over the 150¾ miles from Carlisle to Perth, without any chance of picking up water en route. Although the load was not heavy they had to climb Beattock, and then having passed Stirling they were faced with the long upward pull to Gleneagles. It was a magnificent feat to cover the 150·8 miles from Carlisle to Perth in 149½ minutes. The Webb three-cylinder compound *Adriatic* had a relatively easy task, over the moderate gradients between Euston and Crewe. The Teutonics were easily the best of the Webb compounds, and the only ones that could really run fast. On such occasions one might have expected something better over so fine a road, seeing what the little *Hardwicke* did further north. Even so, an overall time of 148 minutes over the 158·1 miles from Euston to Crewe was not to be despised. It was in any case a record for this stretch that was not surpassed for more than forty years.

So far as the North Western was concerned it was *Hardwicke*'s ascent to Shap that represented such an astonishing output of power in relation to the size of the engine. Working the racing train at 68 to 70mph on level track the engine was developing about 270 to 380 horsepower in the cylinders. Weight for weight that would have been equivalent to about 900 to 1,000 indicated horsepower for a Great Western Castle, or 1,200 to 1,300 for an LMS Duchess – both substantial efforts. But then, when *Hardwicke*'s crew came to the mountain section they stepped up the effort to such an extent that the average speed from Carnforth up to Shap Summit on an average gradient of 1 in 185 was 62·4mph, involving an output of over 600 in the cylinders. This, it may bc added, was the culminating effort after 3,153 miles of racing running since 15 July 1895. On the descent to Carlisle her maximum speeds must have been very near to, if not actually topping, 90mph. No actual maximum speeds were logged on any of the trains on their fastest runs; but from a careful study of the intermediate times I think that the North Eastern 4-4-0 No 1620 would have been somewhere near 90mph on the descent of Cockburnspath bank. Such speeds cannot be definitely claimed, as Charles Rous-Marten and other stop-watching experts were not on the train that night.

Of all the runs made in the closing stages of the 'ninety-five' it is undoubtedly those of the North British between Edinburgh and Dundee that leave a modern traveller bereft of words. During the last week the time over that winding switchback of a line 59·2 miles long with its many restrictions was successively 64¼, 60½ and finally a well-nigh incredible 59 minutes. The risks that must have been taken in negotiating the curves and junctions were incalculable. No doubt the beautifully designed Holmes 4-4-0 locomotives rode very well, and probably gave their crews little anxiety, but it must have been another matter with the six-wheeled coaches. Yet the opinion one forms, after studying contemporary statements of the experiences of passengers, is that the riding was not so rough on the North British as it had been on the North Eastern between Newcastle and Edinburgh. The passing times actually recorded were those at Dalmeny, Kirkcaldy, Thornton and Leuchars Junction; and from these I have attempted to make a reconstruction of the run, from my own considerable experience of running over that route in more recent years, to try to gain some idea of what intermediate speeds were necessary to secure an average speed of 60mph throughout. Of all the records set up in the 'ninety-five', 59 minutes start to stop from Edinburgh to Dundee is the one most likely to stand for all time!

At the points of restricted speed the following can be suggested as likely: 50mph at Inverkeithing, Burntisland and

Thornton; 55mph at Ladybank; 65mph at Cupar and Leuchars Junction; and 60mph upon entering the Tay Bridge. As to likely maximum speeds I would suggest 75mph descending from the Forth Bridge, 80 between Aberdour and Burntisland, 78 before Ladybank, 75 at Springfield, and 72mph at Dairsie and St Fort, and in crossing the Tay Bridge.

A very careful plotting of a graph including all these speeds gives point-to-point averages corresponding with the intermediate times actually recorded; and while one cannot say definitely that these were the speeds actually run I do not think they are very far out. They are indeed enough to make one's hair stand on end, and to make one imagine that the North British were supremely lucky not to sustain a derailment.

When it was all safely over certain remarkable records for high-speed long-distance had been made that can be set out statistically, purely from the viewpoint of speed, without any regard for difficulty of route, train loading, or type of engine:

LONDON AND NORTH WESTERN RAILWAY

Section	*Distance miles*	*Time min*	*Av Speed mph*
Euston–Crewe	158·1	147½	64·3
Crewe–Carlisle	141·1	126	67·2
Euston–Carlisle	299·2	273½ running	65·7
	—	275½ overall	66·2

CALEDONIAN RAILWAY

Section	*Distance miles*	*Time min*	*Av Speed mph*
Carlisle–Perth	150·8	149	60·7
Perth–Aberdeen ticket platform*	89·7	80½	66·8
Carlisle–Aberdeen ticket platform*	240·5	229¾ running	62·8
		232 overall	62·2

* Aberdeen station reached two minutes later

GREAT NORTHERN RAILWAY

Section	*Distance miles*	*Time min*	*Av Speed mph*
Kings Cross–Grantham	105·5	101	62·7
Grantham–York	82·7	76	65·3
Kings Cross–York	188·2	117 running	63·8
		181 overall	62·4

NORTH EASTERN RAILWAY

Section	*Distance miles*	*Time min*	*Av Speed mph*
York–Newcastle	80·6	79	61·2
Newcastle–Edinburgh	124·4	113	66·1
York–Edinburgh	205·0	192 running	64·0
		194 overall	63·4

EAST COAST: Kings Cross–Edinburgh
393·2 miles in overall time of 379 minutes
at an average of 62·2mph

NORTH BRITISH RAILWAY

Section	*Distance miles*	*Time min*	*Av Speed mph*
Edinburgh–Dundee	59·2	59	60·2
Dundee–Aberdeen ticket platform	71·3	76	56·4

How these truly record achievements show up against nineteenth-century performance as a whole is summarised in the next chapter.

CHAPTER FIVE

NINETEENTH CENTURY: A SUMMARY

IT IS no more than natural that with all the excitement and record-breaking of the 'ninety-five' all other British speed achievements in the last decade of the century tend to be obscured. It is also necessary to view these performances in their true perspective, in the light of what had been done prior to the era of outright Anglo-Scottish racing. But before I pass on to a general summary certain runs in other parts of the country must be given a good deal more than a mere passing mention. The 'ninety-five' was not without its repercussions in southern England, and some of those who had to endure the vagaries of the railways running south and south-eastwards from London began writing to the national newspapers contrasting the magnificent performances of the rival Anglo-Scottish routes with what became known as the 'Crawl to the South'. It was the Brighton and South Eastern that became the principal objects of ridicule in a correspondence that vaccillated between rage, contempt and satirical humour. The Chatham also came in for a fair share of adverse comment: the 'Smash 'em and Over' as it was then known!

But while the Brighton seemed afraid to run, and the South Eastern had such a shocking permanent way it dare not, the crack expresses of the Chatham did certainly get a move on, once they were clear of the complicated purlieus of the London suburban area. In June 1896, when the British railway world was astir with much talk of another 'Race to the North', when both the Caledonian and the North Eastern had built 4-4-0 locomotives of considerably increased power to be ready for any eventuality, the Chatham took the opportunity of a special train chartered to take delegates to a conference in Paris to make an exceptionally fast run between Victoria and Dover Pier, in which the 78·4 miles were covered in 81min 56sec start to stop, an average of 57·5mph. Not only this, but on the return trip two days later the special was run almost as rapidly, reaching Victoria in 82min 33sec, although on this occasion it seems that the train started from a point nearer to the shore than that to which the official chainage of Dover Pier station relates. The runs have an added interest in that the load was almost exactly the same as that carried by the West Coast record-breaker on the last night of the 'ninety-five', namely 70 tons. The engine was one of the latest of the Kirtley 4-4-0s of Class M3, with 18in by 26in cylinders and 6ft 6in coupled wheels.

In comparison with the various fast runs made in the 'ninety-five' these very fine Chatham performances are so relatively unknown that abbreviated logs are appended herewith. They certainly represent the records with steam over this route. In later years when the track of the old South Eastern Railway was improved up to the best standards of the day the main line to Folkestone and Dover took its natural place as the principal fast route from London to the Channel Ports; but in the nineteenth century it was completely outclassed by the Chatham.

This relatively high average speed, for anywhere south of the Thames in the nineteenth century, does not appear to have involved any very high maximum speeds. It was achieved by rapid uphill climbing, as from Herne Hill up to Sydenham Hill, on 1 in 100; from Faversham up to Selling, and from Canterbury up to Shepherdswell. The level and well-aligned stretch from New Brompton (now Gillingham) to Faversham produced relatively poor speed for a somewhat large engine, an engine with a light load. The return journey two days later included some considerably faster running on the favourable stretches of line, and an average speed of 71·8mph from Selling to Faversham would almost certainly have involved a maximum of at least 76 or 77mph. The log is appended herewith, but for reasons previously mentioned the initial mileage should be treated with reserve.

LONDON, CHATHAM & DOVER RAILWAY

12 June 1896: Victoria–Dover Pier
Engine: Kirtley Class M3 4-4-0 No 16
Load: 70 tons

Distance miles		*Time min sec*	*Av Speed mph*
0·0	VICTORIA	0 00	—
1·2	Battersea	1 56	37·2
3·9	HERNE HILL	5 10	50·1
5·7	Sydenham Hill	7 24	48·5
8·7	Beckenham	10 35	56·5
10·8	BROMLEY	12 51	55·8
17·6	Swanley	19 53	58·8
26·9	Sole Street	28 56	61·7
32·9	Strood	34 39	63·1
34·4	CHATHAM	36 23	51·8
39·0	Rainham	41 38	52·6
44·7	SITTINGBOURNE	47 03	62·1
52·0	FAVERSHAM	54 25	60·3
55·3	Selling	58 09	52·9
61·8	CANTERBURY	64 49	58·6
71·7	Shepherdswell	74 56	58·8
77·3	Dover Priory	80 14	63·4
78·4	DOVER PIER	81 56	—

By contrast with the foregoing, the South Eastern was severely handicapped by the limitation of maximum speed over the whole line to 60mph. This was perhaps just as well, in view of the state of much of the track. It was only at the very end of the nineteenth century that the Brighton showed

LONDON, CHATHAM & DOVER RAILWAY

14 June 1896: Dover Pier–Victoria
Engine: Kirtley Class M3 4-4-0 No 16
Load: 70 tons

Distance miles		*Time min sec*	*Av Speed mph*
0·0	DOVER PIER	0 00	—
1·1	Dover Priory	1 41	—
6·7	Shepherdswell	9 14	44·5
16·6	CANTERBURY	18 38	63·2
23·1	Selling	25 53	53·8
26·4	FAVERSHAM	28 39	71·8
33·7	SITTINGBOURNE	35 33	63·5
—		pw slack	—
42·5	New Brompton	44 39	58·0
44·0	CHATHAM	46 20	53·4
45·5	Strood	48 08	50·0
51·5	Sole Street	55 39	47·9
57·9	Farningham	61 27	66·2
67·6	BROMLEY	70 28	64·7
72·7	Sydenham Hill	75 45	59·0
74·5	HERNE HILL	77 29	62·0
77·2	Battersea	80 40	50·9
78·4	VICTORIA	82 33	—

some signs of waking up. It was after the 'Crawl to the South' correspondence that an engineer, in more serious vein, wrote to one of the technical journals of the day, making the following comparison:

LONDON & NORTH WESTERN

	Speed
Tebay dep 9.48pm (53 miles) Preston arr 10.55pm	47·4mph

LONDON, BRIGHTON & SOUTH COAST

	Speed
London Bridge dep 5pm	
($50\frac{1}{2}$ miles) Brighton arr 6.5pm	46·6mph

The first was an express fish train from Carlisle to London, and the second was the 'fastest and most wonderful of the Brighton expresses, first class only, at supplementary fares into the bargain'. To which the inimitable E. L. Ahrons added the comment: 'Moral: it is better to be a dead mackerel on the North Western than a first-class passenger on the London, Brighton & South Coast!'

In the autumn of 1898 however the Brighton railway was moved to put on a special Sunday Pullman train, first class only, which ran the 50·9 miles from Victoria to Brighton in the level hour. It was quite a heavy train for the period, weighing 190 tons behind the tender, and the Billinton 4-4-0s of the 1895 class, officially B2, but nicknamed 'Grasshoppers', found some difficulty in keeping time. At that period the 'crack' 8.45am 'Stockbrokers' Express' from Brighton to London Bridge sauntered up in 70 minutes, thus making the startling start-to-stop average of 43·3mph each morning, when it kept time! It is only fair to the London, Brighton & South Coast Railway to add that a great awakening was just around the corner, and that although the company never aspired to high speed in the style of the northern companies there was an all-round smartening-up, accompanied by excellent timekeeping, from the early years of the twentieth century.

The student of railway history and particularly of the development of passenger train services cannot fail to have noticed how completely the Great Western Railway had dropped out of the picture since the halcyon days of broad gauge enterprise in the late 'forties' and early 'fifties'. But with the final abolition of the broad gauge in 1892 a new spirit of enterprise was growing up, and from 1896 the Great Western had the longest non-stop run in Great Britain. It was not regularly made at that time, but only when it was necessary to run the Cornishman in two parts. Then the relief, advance section was run non-stop over the 193·6 miles from Paddington to Exeter in 223 minutes, an average speed of 52·2mph. The Great Western also had the longest regular run then made without stopping, by the 10.18am from Newport to Paddington, via Bath, 143·5 miles at an average speed of 48·6mph. This was then the longest non-stop run made daily anywhere in the world, though the speed was pedestrian compared to what had been achieved between London and Aberdeen in 1895. Nevertheless connoisseurs of Great Western locomotive performance had not been slow to notice that the Dean 7ft 6in 4-2-2 singles were very free-running engines, and before the end of the century Charles Rous-Marten had recorded a maximum speed of 83½mph with one of them down the Wellington bank, between Whiteball tunnel and Taunton. Although this was a mere foretaste of what was to come on the Great Western in a few years' time, that maximum of 83½mph does appear to be the highest authentically recorded on the line up to the end of the century.

As that time approached it seemed that the maximum speed record would be held by the North Eastern by the J class 7ft 7in 4-2-2s in their short-lived conditions as compounds. There was the extraordinary output of over 1,000 indicated horsepower at 86mph by engine No 1518, and the maximum of 90mph attained by No 1517 on test. But then S. W. Johnson's supremely beautiful 7ft 9in 4-2-2s of the 115 class took the road in 1896. It was very soon evident that they were extremely fast engines. The long descent from the thirty-fourth milepost out of St Pancras extending for nearly 15 miles, and inclined mostly at 1 in 200, is an ideal place for the making of speed records, and these engines had not long been in service before Charles Rous-Marten logged an exceptionally fast run with No 117. For 13 consecutive miles the speed was over 80mph and the maximum was a full 90mph. From what Rous-Marten wrote subsequently however it would seem that the running conditions had been particularly favourable on this occasion. Several times afterwards, with the enthusiastic co-operation of the driver, attempts were made to repeat this performance with engine No 117; but the maximum they could get was 86mph. From my own experience of getting drivers to co-operate in attempting very high speeds I fancy that, on the occasion of that memorable and indisputable 90, engine No 117 must have been like the Lord High Executioner of Titipu, 'wafted by a favouring gale'! It is certainly astonishing what an adverse or favourable wind can do when it comes to exceptionally fast running.

So the nineteenth century came to an end with two single-wheelers sharing the maximum speed honours: No 1517 of the North Eastern, and No 117 of the Midland, bracketed equal with a maximum of 90mph. As I remarked in the last chapter, however, it is probable that maximum speeds of 90mph and perhaps more were attained during the 'ninety-five'; but no one was on board with a stop watch to record such maxima precisely. So far as authentic records go the third place goes to the little North Western Precedent No 2002 *Madge*. She was working a heavy up Anglo-Scottish express loaded to 211 tons tare, and somewhat naturally took a pilot from Carlisle up to Shap Summit. From the restart she passed Carnforth 31·4 miles in 28min 26sec – a start-to-pass average of 66·3mph – and in the course of this hurricane descent Rous-Marten recorded a sustained maximum speed of 88½mph. I have mentioned in Chapter Four the speed-worthiness of the three-cylinder compounds of the Teutonic class. Mr Bowen-Cooke himself recorded a maximum speed of 87mph with one of these engines on the descent from Whitmore towards Stafford; but another of these engines, No 1306 *Ionic*, made a nineteenth-century record that in its way was as fine as the high-speed achievements of other London & North Western locomotives.

Having run the length of the main line from Euston to Carlisle at an average speed of 65·3mph on the last night of the race the North Western then proceeded to demonstrate that they could run that 299·2 mile stretch non-stop. It was a record of a kind no other British railway could touch, unless the Great Western attempted to extend the Exeter non-stop into Cornwall, and in 1895 that would have been most unlikely. The North Western effort was purely a demonstration, with a special train weighing 151 tons tare. It was a sure sign that the strong Sabbatarian hand of Sir Richard Moon no longer reigned in the chairman's room at Euston, because the trip was made on Sunday 1 September 1895. It was necessary to use Crewe men, as being the only depot at which the top-link express drivers knew the road both to Euston and to Carlisle; and who better than the pair who made such a magnificent record with *Hardwicke* on the last night of the race, Driver Robinson and Fireman Wolstencroft. Naturally no attempt at a speed record was made. The old wooden-framed tenders that were then standard did not carry all that much coal; and while it was one thing to fire at maximum intensity for two hours, as Wolstencroft did in the race, it was quite another thing to be at the shovel for nearly six hours at a stretch. The train left Euston at 8.45am and reached Carlisle after a steady and uneventful run at 2.38pm – 299·2 miles in 353 minutes, an average of 51mph. It remained the British long-distance non-stop record until 1928.

There was nevertheless more to it than a piece of showmanship. After the race there was a great deal of discussion among the East Coast managements as to how further acceleration could be made, and there was more than one suggestion of cutting out intermediate stops. On paper this is undoubtedly one way of cutting end-to-end times, if the tenders can be replenished en route from water troughs. But on a very long run other considerations enter in. There is the mundane matter of getting coal forward. In the early days of the Exeter non-stops Great Western firemen were glad enough to take advantage of the long slowing over the Bristol avoiding line to go into the tender and get coal forward.

If the fireman was having difficulties in this respect, and was tiring from the sheer labour of his task, the driver might be forced to ease up, and the slower subsequent running could easily wipe all advantage derived from not making an intermediate stop. I shall always remember my first footplate run on one of the Carlisle–Euston non-stop runs, in 1934, when we got into trouble for this very reason. It was tolerably certain that if we had been able to stop for three or four minutes at Crewe to get a good supply of coal forward we could have made a faster end-to-end time than we actually did non-stop! The difference between the combined efforts of *Adriatic* and *Hardwicke* on the night of 22 August 1895 and the non-stop run of *Ionic* on 1 September points its own moral: 65·3mph against 51mph.

The summer of 1896 saw the new Caledonian 4-4-0s of the first Dunalastair class showing magnificent form on the train that had done the racing a year earlier. In the north the schedules had remained very fast for non-racing conditions, such as 112 minutes for the 105·3 miles from Wigan to Carlisle on the LNWR, and 125 minutes for the 117·8 miles from Carlisle to Stirling. These averages of 56·5mph on both stages would appear to involve very hard work, when the loads conveyed were regularly between two and a half and three times the weight of the racing train on the last night of the contest. On the North Western the train was almost invariably double-headed with a pair of 2-4-0s, because although the Teutonics were taking loads of nearly 300 tons unassisted over Shap there were only ten of them, and one was usually reserved at that time for the afternoon West Coast Corridor train. On the Caledonian, however, the new Dunalastairs made the very fast schedule of the night Tourist express look easy with loads of up to 200 tons. All one can say is 'Woe betide the East Coast if there *had* been another race!' The logs of four runs tell their own tale. The first two are the fastest runs in the 1888 and 1895 races, and the third and fourth are ordinary runs made on the Tourist express in 1896.

Run No	1	2	3	4
Engine No	123	90	728	733
Load tons	80	72	170	180
Distance miles	*Time m s*	*Time m s*	*Time m s*	*Time m s*
0·0 Carlisle	0 00	0 00	0 00	0 00
25·8 Lockerbie	26 46	27 00	25 59	25 50
39·7 Beattock	39 13	39 30	37 50	38 23
49·7 Summit	53 04	53 00	53 33	53 30
66·9 Symington	69 04	68 00	67 44	68 24
94·3 Coatbridge	To	—	94 13	94 29
117·8 Stirling	Edinburgh	116 30*	116 53	117 40

* Passing time

It will be seen that there was very little in it, so far as times go; and in relation to the loads hauled the Drummond 4-4-0 No 90 on the last night of the 'ninety-five' made a relatively poor showing. But as I have explained in the previous chapter, Driver Crooks was, for the first time in Caledonian history, attempting a non-stop run to Perth, and was nursing his engine to a considerable extent. By contrast the performances of the Dunalastairs only a year later was astounding by any standards. The driver of No 728 was Tom Robinson, who with the Drummond engine No 78 had shared the working of the racer with Crooks a year earlier. To him stood the record for the start-to-stop run from Carlisle to Stirling during the race when he covered the 117·8 miles in 114 minutes. This run in itself was a good instance of the suggestion that cutting out stops does not necessarily shorten the overall time. On this occasion there was a stop of 2 minutes at Stirling, and then No 78 and her crew were so fortified by that brief pause that the remaining 33 miles on to Perth were covered in 34 minutes start to stop. The running time from Carlisle was thus 148 minutes, and the total

150, against the 149½ minutes run non-stop, and in the circumstances of considerable anxiety on the final night of the race.

In the year after the race however it is the Dunalastairs and not the Drummonds that claim attention; and here were the new engines not merely equalling but surpassing the racing times, with more than double the loads. What they might have done with the loads of the 'ninety-five' rather staggers the imagination; but no resumption of racing took place in 1896, and when autumn came the Tourist express was decelerated, and never again reached the level of speed scheduled in that memorable summer. The Dunalastairs were extremely fast engines too. One of them gave Charles Rous-Marten a sustained maximum speed of 85½mph descending the Clyde valley with the Tourist express, and this remained an all-time record for the Caledonian Railway. It was not until LMS days that this speed was surpassed.

Before turning to a final summary of the speed achievements of the nineteenth century I must mention what is surely a record weight-hauling performance – of all the greater significance in that weight-hauling rather than exceptionally high speed was to be the principal feature of British express train running during the first twenty years of the twentieth century. The train was the up West Coast corridor dining car express, which for many years was worked, day in day out, between Euston and Crewe by the Teutonic class three-cylinder compound No 1304 *Jeanie Deans*. Whatever trains might be double-headed on the North Western in those days the Corridor stood apart. It was a point of honour with the two drivers who shared the working never to take a pilot if No 1304 was on the job. At a time when 150 to 200 tons was a normally heavy load for an express train, two runs were recorded from Crewe to Euston on which the tare loads were 312 and 326 tons behind the tender, representing gross trailing loads of about 335 and 350 tons. These were enormous loads for the period, and with them *Jeanie Deans* made the following remarkable runs:

CREWE–WILLESDEN

3-cylinder compound No 1304 *Jeanie Deans*

Section	*Distance miles*	*335 tons*		*350 tons*	
		Time m s	*Av Speed mph*	*Time m s*	*Av Speed mph*
Crewe–Nuneaton	61·0	71 39	51·1	71 30	51·2
Nuneaton–Willesden	91·7	103 17	53·3	101 54	54·0

Both were good, but the second is really quite astonishing, especially seeing that the maximum speed never quite reached 70mph at any point. On the other hand the 15 entirely adverse miles from Bletchley to Tring took no more than 17min 40sec. As usual the train was running well on time. It would have been most interesting to see what overall time could have been made if the driver had used the well-proven high-speed capabilities of the Teutonics to full advantage in running downhill from Roade to Castlethorpe troughs, or from Tring down to Wembley – or Sudbury, as the station was then known. High speed or not, the working of a 350-ton train over a distance of 91·7 miles at an average speed of 54mph, without exceeding 70mph, is one of the most convincing demonstrations of the power of these engines that one could ever wish for. The extraordinary thing is that Webb, their own designer, did not seem to appreciate how near he was to an absolute winner with these engines. He built no more than ten, and then veered away to the freakish Greater Britains, and followed them with those monumental sluggards, the Jubilee and Alfred the Great 4-4-0 compounds.

Now we come to the nineteenth-century summary. I must

admit that it is with a little hesitancy that I set down the following tabulations to be claimed as out-and-out records. The early speed history of the railways of Great Britain is not lavishly documented; and although a good deal of research lies behind the tabulations presented this is not to say that other records may at some time be unearthed. The authorities are mainly Rous-Marten and E. L. Ahrons, supplemented by official and test records quoted by Sir Daniel Gooch, Walter M. Smith (North Eastern Railway), C. J. Bowen-Cooke, and W. F. Pettigrew, in respect of the Adams 7ft 4-4-0. The records of running in the races of 1888 and 1895 are taken from my own book *Railway Race to the North*, which was the result of a great amount of research in the years 1956 and 1957.

MAXIMUM RECORDED SPEEDS, OVER 80 MPH

Speed mph	*Railway*	*Engine No and class*
90	NER	Class J No 1517 4-2-2 2cyl compound
90	Midland	7ft 9in 4-2-2 No 117
88¼	LNWR	6ft 6in 2-4-0 No 2002 *Madge*
87	LNWR	3cyl compound No 1309 *Adriatic*
86½	GNR	Stirling 7ft 6in 2-2-2
85½	Caledonian	Dunalastair I class 4-4-0
85	GNR	Stirling 8ft 4-2-2
83½	GWR	Dean 7ft 8in 4-2-2
81¾	Midland	Kirtley 800 class 2-4-0
81¾	GWR	Broad Gauge 4-2-2 *Lightning*
81	LSWR	Adams 7ft 4-4-0
81	NER	M class 4-4-0 No 1621
80½	Midland	6ft 9in 4-4-0 No 1563

The above table includes only definite published recordings. It is fairly certain that in addition the North Eastern M class 4-4-0 No 1620 reached speeds that are best described as 85plus mph on the last night of the 'ninety-five'. Her probable speeds include an average of 80mph from Belford to Beal, and of 81mph from Cockburnspath to Innerwick. But these figures arose from an attempted reconstruction of a detailed log, with no more facts to work upon than the passing times actually recorded at Belford, Berwick, Reston, Dunbar, Drem, and Longniddry. From those the averages work out at 76·6mph from Belford to Berwick, 68·5mph from Dunbar to Drem, and 78·8mph on to Longniddry. There was probably another maximum of 80mph on this latter stretch, and Rous-Marten clocked an 81 in the approach to Portobello with engine No 1621 of the same class two days earlier. This is the figure included in the table. On this run the Rev W. J. Scott reported a maximum of 80mph down the Cockburnspath bank. I will not dwell upon the possibilities of very high maximum speeds with *Hardwicke* on the descent from Shap to Carlisle, because we already have the record of 88¼mph with *Madge.* I can only leave the chronicle of nineteenth-century maximum speeds at that.

Next comes a table of fast start-to-stop runs, and these I have put in roughly chronological order. From this it will be seen that by the odd decimal point or two *Hardwicke* claims the honour of the fastest start-to-stop run up to the end of the century. However, it must be borne in mind that the times handed down to us for the majority of these old runs were taken to nothing more accurate than the nearest half-minute; and a half a minute either way could turn the scale of priorities. All one can really say by way of conclusion is that *Hardwicke*, the Lambie 4-4-0 No 17 and the North Eastern 4-4-0 No 1620 were all roughly on a level, and level moreover with Gooch's old records of 1846 and 1848. The new century was however not many years old before a new and entirely precise record was set up for the fastest British start-to-stop run ever made.

Although many of the reports left by nineteenth-century

observers are tantalizingly vague, research into railway speed records is fascinating to the last degree, and one feels that the time is still far away when it can be said that the last piece of evidence has been unearthed.

Year	*Railway*	*Section*	*Distance miles*	*Time min*	*Av Speed mph*	*Class of Locomotive*
1846 & 1848	GWR broad gauge	Paddington–Didcot	53·1	47½	67·0	2-2-2 (1846) 4-2-2 (1848)
1847	LNWR	Wolverton–Coventry	41·0	42	58·6	Long-boilered 3cyl 4-2-0
1848	Midland	Derby–Altofts Junc.	63·6	68	56·0	Jenny Lind 2-2-2
1862	LNWR	Holyhead–Trent Valley Junction	130·5	144	54·3	Lady of the Lake 2-2-2 *Watt*
1862	LNWR	Trent Valley Junction–Euston	133·1	139½	57·2	Extra-large Bloomer No 372
1888	LNWR	Euston–Crewe	158·1	166	57·1	Lady of the Lake 2-2-2 *Waverley*
1888	LNWR	Preston–Carlisle	90·1	90	60·0	Precedent 2-4-0 *Vulcan*
1888	Caledonian	Carlisle–Edinburgh	100·6	102½	58·8	4-2-2 No. 123
1888	GNR	Kings Cross–Grantham	105·5	105	60·3	Stirling 2-2-2 No 233
1888	NER	York–Newcastle	80·6	78	62·0	Tennant 2-4-0 No 1475
1895	GNR	Kings Cross–Grantham	105·5	101	62·7	Stirling 4-2-2 No 668
1895	GNR	Grantham–York	82·7	76	65·3	Stirling 4-2-2 No 775
1895	NER	Newcastle–Edinburgh	124·4	113	66·1	M class 4-4-0 No 1620
1895	NBR	Edinburgh–Dundee	59·2	59	60·2	Holmes 4-4-0 No 293

Year	*Railway*	*Section*	*Distance miles*	*Time min*	*Av Speed mph*	*Class of Locomotive*
1895	LNWR	Euston–Crewe	158·1	147½	64·3	3cyl compound *Adriatic*
1895	LNWR	Crewe–Carlisle	141·1	126	67·2	Precedent 2-4-0 *Hardwicke*
1895	Caledonian	Carlisle–Stirling	117·8	114	62·0	Drummond 4-4-0 No 78
1895	Caledonian	Carlisle–Perth	150·8	149	60·7	Drummond 4-4-0 No 90
1895	Caledonian	Perth–Aberdeen*	89·7	80½	66·8	Lambie 4-4-0 No 17
1895	LNWR	Euston–Carlisle	299·2	353	50·8	3cyl compound *Ionic*
1896	LCDR	Victoria–Dover Pier	78·4	82	57·3	Kirtley 4-4-0 No 16

* Ticket platform

CHAPTER SIX

OCEAN MAILS

WHEN MAN sets his mind on the breaking of records and prestige becomes involved, the logic of commerce and of everyday life is apt to go through the window! G. P. Neele, Superintendent of the Line of the London & North Western Railway during the 'ninety-five' and on the point of retiring, wrote, in his famous reminiscences:

> Now there was really nothing gained by the arrival at 6.25 or 6.30 in Aberdeen. The hotels were not open for their regular work; the discomfort of unprepared breakfast tables, or the accompaniment of dusting damsels in the coffee rooms, were travellers' annoyances rather than conveniences. The hour earlier into Aberdeen was a drawback rather than a benefit. However, after the end of July it ceased to be any part of my duty.

One feels that Neele was jolly glad to be out of it. Arrivals at 6.30 indeed; three weeks later both sides were tearing into Aberdeen before 5am! But if such early arrivals in Aberdeen were an inconvenience, to put it mildly, how can one describe in any logical terms the well-nigh incredible situation that developed in 1904 over the working of the inward-bound American traffic from Plymouth to London?

On each arrival from the USA there was tacit agreement that the London & South Western Railway should take the London passengers, and that the Great Western should take the mails. The latter company, then travelling to London via

Bristol, was well placed to give an excellent service for north-country mails as well as those for London. One can certainly appreciate the desirability of providing as rapid a delivery as possible for all incoming American mail, and dispatching the special trains as soon as possible after the arrival of the steamer; but it was surely another matter for the passengers. Would they appreciate a very fast railway journey to be landed in London in the small hours of the morning? Of course it must be remembered that the ships making the Atlantic crossing were German, and that Plymouth was no more than a brief port of call. There could be no staying comfortably on board, and then landing at some reasonable hour. Landing had to be made as soon as the steamer dropped anchor in Plymouth Sound. With the likelihood of night as well as day journeys the London & South Western Railway had sleeping cars available, and one can appreciate the argument 'Better get these folks to London rather than keep them hanging about in Plymouth.'

How the arrival of each steamer from the USA became the starting signal for an undisguised race to London between the mail and the passenger train is a long story. The South Western was intent upon giving an immaculate service to a clientele containing a high proportion of first-class passengers. Many of these would be travelling further into continental Europe, and the South Western considered it a matter of high prestige to create the best possible impression of British express train travelling. There seems very little doubt that the race developed from a certain amount of coat trailing by the Great Western. That company entered into the twentieth century in a spirit of boundless enterprise, and an enthusiasm that bade fair to eclipse even the most ambitious days of Brunel, Gooch and the broad gauge. The company had for too long been forced to play a passive rôle in the evolution of British railway engineering and operation; and those who had the spirit of Brunel and Gooch in their hearts must have looked on rather wistfully while the East and West Coast routes to the north were so covering themselves with glory in the 'ninety-five'. Even before the storm of 1904 broke with all its vigour upon the hitherto placid shires of the West Country there had been clear evidence of the new spirit of enterprise in the running of Great Western express trains.

Although William Dean was still firmly in the saddle at Swindon connoisseurs of locomotive practice had been quick to notice a growing change in the outward appearance of Great Western locomotives, from the exquisitely proportioned 7ft 8in 4-2-2 singles to the somewhat angular Badminton 4-4-0s, and then to the brutally functional Atbaras. It was nevertheless pointed out that similar if perhaps not so drastic changes were taking place elsewhere on British railways, and in particular that the elegant nineteenth-century lines of Midland locomotives were considerably changed in S. W. Johnson's Belpaire 4-4-0s of 1901. We now know, of course, that the new Great Western 4-4-0s, and particularly the Atbaras, were the outward and visible sign of a mighty new power behind the throne at Swindon in the person of George Jackson Churchward. This is no place to discuss the inner history of the Locomotive Department at this period in time, or to dilate upon the design features of the Atbara class 4-4-0s. It is enough to say that they were the fastest and probably the most economical locomotives yet to run on British metals. Their speedworthiness paved the way for the establishment of new standards of running on level track. Hitherto the general yardstick of express train speed in Great Britain had been a sustained 60mph on the level. Rous-Marten and others had secured the co-operation of drivers in attempting to secure high maximum speeds; but all these efforts had been downhill, as from Stoke box down to Peterborough on the Great Northern, Leagrave down to Bedford on the Midland, and down Wellington bank on the Great Western. Now Churchward was setting new targets of performance on level track.

In 1901 the Great Western had seventeen daily runs of 100 miles or more made non-stop. The longest was still that from Paddington to Exeter, 193·6 miles, then made in 218 minutes at an average speed of 53·2mph, and the fastest was that of the Birmingham non-stops, via Oxford, which covered the 129·3 miles in 143 minutes, at an average speed of 54·2mph. Many of these workings were entrusted to single-wheelers, and in bad rail conditions or inclement weather no little difficulty was experienced in keeping time. The advent of the Badminton and Atbara 4-4-0s began to change all that, though at first there were not enough of these excellent 4-4-0s to work all the long-distance high speed trains. There was nevertheless a high prestige value set upon the operation of long non-stop runs, and opportunity to make their longest yet came to the Great Western in 1902. In March of that year King Edward VII and Queen Alexandra made a tour of the West Country, and the tour began with the running of the Royal Train non-stop from Paddington to Kingswear, 228·5 miles. For the train of five saloons one of the Atbara class engines was used, No 3374, which was specially named *Britannia* for the occasion. A splendid run was made. To Exeter, passed in 206½ minutes from Paddington, the average speed was 56·2mph, but the slow running thereafter, over single line sections, brought the overall average to Kingswear down to 52·2mph. At the conclusion of the tour the GWR went one better, and ran the Royal Train non-stop from Millbay Junction to Paddington 264·4 miles in 284 minutes, another very commendable average speed of 52·1mph. This was not only the longest non-stop run yet attempted on the Great Western, but also the longest that had been made with a Royal Train. The same engine was used, namely No 3374 *Britannia.*

Both runs require special notice: the down journey as being the only occasion on which the entire route from Paddington to Kingswear had been made non-stop, and the up journey in the prelude it provided to the inauguration of regular non-stop running between Paddington and Plymouth in 1904. The Royal Train made an even longer run than that regularly scheduled afterwards, because it started from Millbay Junction instead of from North Road. Both runs are certainly records of their own kind, and their logs are appended herewith:

ROYAL TRAIN

Friday 7 March 1902
Load: 5 coaches, 135 tons full
Engine: 4-4-0 No 3374 *Britannia*

Distance miles		*Time min*	*Av Speed mph*
0·0	Paddington	0	—
31·0	Twyford	34	54·7
36·2	*Reading West Box*	39	62·4
53·1	Didcot	56	59·6
77·3	Swindon	80	60·5
106·9	Bath	110½	58·2
118·4	*Pylle Hill Junction*	127	44·5
137·7	*Uphill Junction*	146	61·0
162·8	Taunton	171½	59·0
193·6	Exeter	206½	52·0
213·8	Newton Abbot	234½	43·2
228·5	Kingswear	262½	31·5

It will be seen that no attempt at exceptionally fast running was made, and instead a steady average of 60mph was sustained on the open road. The above timings are taken from the official record of the trip. On the return journey on 10 March the running was very similar, with an average speed of 55·6mph from passing Exeter to the top at Paddington. The overall average was a little higher than that of the North Western run with the *Ionic* from Euston to Carlisle; but it was one thing to make a very long run with a private special and quite another to attempt the company's longest non-stop up to that time with the King and Queen on board! That it was done very successfully was a great feather in the cap of the Great Western Railway.

ROYAL TRAIN

Monday 10 March 1902
Load: 5 coaches, 135 tons full
Engine: 4-4-0 No 3374 *Britannia*

Distance miles		*Time min*	*Av Speed mph*
0·0	Millbay Junction	0	—
32·6	Newton Abbot	47	41·7
52·8	Exeter	75	43·2
83·6	Taunton	109½	53·6
108·7	*Uphill Junction*	137	54·8
129·4	*Bristol East Depot*	159½	55·3
139·5	Bath	172	48·5
169·1	Swindon	203	57·3
193·4	*Didcot East*	227	60·7
210·2	*Reading West Box*	245½	54·5
215·4	Twyford	251	56·7
246·4	Paddington	284	56·3

What delighted the Great Western authorities was the evident personal interest taken by the King in all the railway arrangements. It seemed that he regarded the journeys to and from the West Country as much a part of the tour as the numerous engagements he and the Queen fulfilled when in Devonshire. There was every reason to be proud of the railways of Great Britain at that time. Although France and America could boast of some start-to-stop runs faster than our best the British railways were the busiest in the world, and incomparably the safest. Railways were still the pre-eminent means of travelling by land, and this Royal interest and encouragement to do even better was to have a striking sequel just over a year later.

Once again it was the Great Western Railway that had the opportunity to show its mettle. It was not the King himself this time, but the Prince of Wales (afterwards King George V), who with the Princess of Wales was travelling to Cornwall for a visit to the estates and lands of the Royal Duchy.

Arrangements were made to convey the party by the ordinary Cornishman express; but 'a good run' had been asked for in very high quarters, and so three saloons allocated to the Royal party were run on an advance portion of the train – moreover, non-stop from Paddington to Plymouth North Road. It is evident that a very special effort was planned well in advance, and so that the results should be widely publicized, in the most impartial manner, the managements took the unusual step of inviting two distinguished exponents of the stop-watch, Charles Rous-Marten and the Rev W. J. Scott, to travel by the train. A reserved compartment in one of the two ordinary coaches was put at their disposal. One of the latest 4-4-0 locomotives having the Churchward taper boiler was put on to the job – No 3433 *City of Bath* – and so at 10.40am on 14 July 1903 they set out on the first-ever non-stop run in the down direction between Paddington and Plymouth. The load of 130 tons was not heavy by later standards, but reckoning the tender with the train the engine itself was hauling just over three times its own weight, almost exactly the same proportion as *Hardwicke,* and the Great Northern eight-foot bogie singles in the 'ninety-five', but greater than that of the North Eastern and Caledonian 4-4-0s, the ratios of which were 2·8 and 2·46 respectively. The performance of the *City of Bath* can therefore be compared on level or slightly advantageous terms to the spectacular achievements of eight years earlier.

Scott and Rous-Marten had been given no hint of what was proposed. Scott wrote afterwards:

> Some of us favoured some weeks ahead with an invitation for this run hoped for much, but not the most

daringly hopeful dreamed of reaching Exeter inside of three hours, still less of getting to Plymouth well under four. Before Slough was reached, hope gave place to pleased surprise, which grew to wonder by Reading, and amazement at Didcot, when even the phantom record of the old BG days was 'cut'.

Getting away from Paddington smartly .speed indeed settled down to a steady 70 to 73mph all the way from West Drayton, and the average for the 39·9 miles on to Didcot was exactly 72mph. The actual time passing through Didcot was 47min 33sec, equalling though not cutting the old broad-gauge record. But the actual speeds run by the *City of Bath* show that nothing very exceptional would have been needed from Daniel Gooch's *Great Britain* on the form those engines were then showing. But so far as the *City of Bath* was concerned it was merely a beginning. The same kind of speed was maintained steadily up the gradual rise through the Vale of the White Horse, and having passed Swindon in 68min 1sec the engine was taken at full tilt down Dauntsey bank to attain a maximum speed of 87mph.

By that time there was every sign that the engine had settled into a perfectly steady stride. Churchward's taper boiler was steaming with the constancy that I myself saw in it in later years on so many different classes of Great Western locomotives, from Bulldogs and the rejuvenated *City of Truro,* to Halls, Castles, and Kings. In *City of Bath*'s case that 87mph down Dauntsey bank came as a matter of course, not like some of the maxima secured by Rous-Marten in earlier days and recorded in the previous chapter. At Chippenham the average speed from the start was 69·5mph, but unlike so many occasions in the 'ninety-five' no attempt was made to gain further time by running faster than usual through areas of restricted speed. Due caution was shown in passing through Bath, and on the lengthy negotiation of the Bristol avoiding line. Despite this caution the train passed over Pylle Hill Junction and re-entered the main line in just under the even 1¾ hours from Paddington. In other words the celebrated schedule of the Bristolian of 1935 had been slightly better.

It was, however, after Bristol that the run began to partake of a more truly record nature. After mounting the rise to Flax Bourton and descending through Nailsea, the speed settled down to a steady 75–6mph, and the average over the 21·3 miles from Yatton to Bridgwater was 75·2mph. It is true that both Caledonian and North Eastern 4-4-0s had run at closely comparative speeds on level track during the 'ninety-five', but in the course of much shorter runs. The extreme significance of the running of the *City of Bath* between Bristol and Taunton was that not only had the fastest time in history just been made between Paddington and Bristol, but that following this tremendous sprint across the levels of Somersetshire there still remained the fearsome gradients of the South Devon line, all to be taken in the course of a non-stop run of nearly 250 miles! It can therefore be reasonably inferred that 75mph was the ideal cruising speed of the locomotive on level track when hauling three times its own weight. On passing Taunton the average speed from the start was 68·6mph. At that time there was a moderate speed restriction through the old covered-in station at Taunton; but recovery was vigorous, and the Wellington bank was climbed in magnificent style, with speed not falling below 50mph. It would have been interesting to see what kind of maximum speeds would have been attained on the long descent to Exeter had the engine been allowed to run, as she had been at Dauntsey; but the Royal party were then at lunch, and the driver was instructed to run a little more easily. In consequence speed averaged no more than 66mph from Whiteball to Exeter. Even so, Exeter was passed in the remarkable time of 172min 34sec from Paddington – an average speed of 67·5mph and 32½ minutes ahead of the normal time of this express.

Record breaking certainly continued after Exeter, but of a different kind. A comparison between miles, minutes and seconds reveals nothing very striking, because the 52 miles to North Road station, Plymouth, took 61 minutes and one second pass to stop. This can be amply explained by the very difficult character of the route. While the Dainton and Rattery inclines between them account for no more than 7 out of those 52 miles the incessant curves impose constant restraint on the running, added to which there remained at that time one single-line section, between Dawlish and Teignmouth, involving slacks for staff exchange at each end. Added to all this was the very severe speed restriction through Newton Abbot station. The only part of the South Devon line where one can really get a run is between Exeter and the point where the coast is reached, about midway between Exminster and Starcross. The *City of Bath* was worked up to nearly 80mph on this stretch, but then was most heavily restrained. It is nevertheless significant of the physical handicaps imposed by the curvature of this line that today, with two Warship class diesel-hydraulic locomotives provided to work the nine-coach Cornish Riviera Express, the scheduled time between Exeter and Plymouth is now 70 minutes. From experience on the footplate I can testify that with close observation of all the speed restrictions now prescribed there is very little time in hand!

In 1903, by running that last 52-mile stretch in the level hour Plymouth was reached in the utterly unprecedented time of 3 hours 53 minutes 35 seconds – faster than anything subsequently scheduled in steam days, and via Bristol into the bargain! The overall average speed was 63·4mph, a record for this distance that was not to be surpassed for more than thirty years. Such an achievement naturally set all railway enthusiasts of the day agog. 'Railwayacs' they were known at that time; and the Rev. W. J. Scott calculated that on similar form the Great Northern ought to have been able to run the 188·2 miles from Kings Cross to York in 168min start to stop. If, he argued, the North Eastern continued the good work and made a non-stop run from York to Edinburgh, using, when it was completed, the King Edward

Bridge over the Tyne and running through Newcastle without stopping, no more than 186 minutes should have been necessary for the 204·5 miles. This would have left 6 minutes for changing engines at York, and given a six-hour schedule from London to Edinburgh. But no one on the northern lines took the hint!

This run in July 1903, and the approbation it received from so many quarters, gave the Great Western immense confidence in their new locomotives. By that time, of course, the new Churchward 4-6-0s were beginning to appear from Swindon Works; but as yet they were experimental. The main burden of the express train service was being borne by the Atbaras and the new Cities – aided, of course, by the Dean 7ft 8in 4-2-2 singles. The record run of 14 July had sent a tremendous surge of pride through the whole service, and when the new Ocean Mail traffic began to develop, and there was agreement to share a part of it with the London & South Western, there can be little doubt there were many on the Great Western side who determined that whatever else might happen they would not be second to the South Western where speed was concerned. In this, of course, the extra distance to be covered was a challenge, as it had been to the West Coast Route in the 'ninety-five'. The South Western were nevertheless at a disadvantage in Plymouth. The passengers were landed at Stonehouse Pool Quay, where an excellent Ocean Terminal Station had been laid out; but then the boat train had to be hauled for half a mile up the branch to the junction with the main line, where the express engine would be waiting, and the direction of travel reversed. It was usually eight or nine minutes after leaving the Quay before the express started away in earnest.

The distance from Stonehouse Pool Junction to Exeter St Davids is 57·6 miles, compared to 52·9 miles from Millbay Dock Gates by the Great Western route; so that with an equivalent average speed when on the run the Great Western had a potential ten minutes in hand over this part of the journey to set against the 20 miles of extra distance from

Exeter to London. At Exeter, of course, there was a potential Kinnaber, for the South Western route intersected the Great Western for almost 1½ miles, from Cowley Bridge Junction to St Davids station. There was always the possibility that the rival trains might be offered simultaneously to the signalmen at Cowley Bridge, for one to cross over in front of the other. As to their respective chances, while in general the South Western were new to the game it must not be forgotten that in Dugald Drummond they had a Chief Mechanical Engineer who had been on the Caledonian during the 'eighty-eight', and whose 4-4-0 engines had greatly distinguished themselves in the 'ninety-five'.

The South Western laboured from the outset under the mysticism of omitting stops, in order to save time, and evolved the extraordinary procedure of changing engines at Templecombe. This not only entailed a long and difficult run from Stonehouse Pool Junction, with the anxiety of water supply in the absence of water troughs; but involved a non-stop run from Templecombe to Waterloo, with what proved to be a hazardous non-stop passage through Salisbury. Drummond used his new large-boilered 6ft 4-4-0s to facilitate the hill-climbing west of Exeter, but these engines were hardly ideal for the high-speed running east of Exeter. I am sure that faster overall times could have been made if engines had been changed at Exeter and Salisbury, and the T9 4-4-0s run in their own uninhibited style on the 88 and 83·6 mile stretches customary in the ordinary West of England express workings of the period. On the inaugural day of South Western participation in the ocean traffic the 6ft 4-4-0 No 399 made a relatively poor run to Templecombe, even allowing for unpremeditated stops; but the T9 4-4-0 No 336 made some fast running onwards to Waterloo, covering the 112·2 miles in 110 minutes 25 seconds despite a stop at the 91st milepost requested by Dugald Drummond himself. After Salisbury the 60·8 miles from Grateley to Surbiton were covered in 52min 40sec, an average of 69·6mph.

The fastest South Western run on record was made on 23

April 1904, when Charles Rous-Marten was a passenger. The T9 class 4-4-0 No 336 was again on the job, with a load of four coaches, 105 tons behind the tender. The following is an abridged log of the journey:

TEMPLECOMBE–WATERLOO

Distance miles		*Time m s*	*Av Speed mph*
0·0	Templecombe	0 00	—
28·4	Salisbury	28 03	60·8
45·8	Andover	45 09	61·1
64·4	Basingstoke	62 00	66·2
79·0	Farnborough	74 13	71·8
87·8	Woking	81 49	70·0
100·2	Surbiton	92 30	69·7
108·3	Clapham Junction	99 39	68·0
112·2	Waterloo	104 33	47·8

The average speed was thus 64·5mph, but having regard to the light load the performance was not very exciting. After all, the stretch from Basingstoke to Surbiton was almost entirely favourable, and the average speed of only 70·5mph does not appear very enterprising by comparison with what Drummond's older engines had done on the Caledonian nine years earlier. The extraordinary feature of South Western working of that period is the speed at which they seemed regularly to run through Salisbury. These American Specials were the only passenger trains that passed Salisbury without stopping, and from the very first day of the service scant regard seems to have been paid to the exceedingly awkward layout at the east end of the station. If it had been no more than a curve the conditions would have been little different from many taken at high speed in the 'ninety-five', between Newcastle and Dundee; but on that curve at Salisbury there was a crossover to the left, which quite properly was subject to a speed limit of 25mph. Yet in describing the run of 23 April Rous-Marten wrote:

> At Templecombe West No 336, already referred to, replaced No 399, and the driver (F. Gare) from the first evidently had set his heart upon record-breaking. We ran through Salisbury station at full speed, and after obtaining a very high maximum down the descent at 1 in 165...

from Grateley of course.

It seems incredible that no one appreciated the terrible risks that were being taken at this location – why, Heaven knows! If the running east of Basingstoke had been in the style of *Hardwicke*, or NER No 1620, one could have seen it fitted into a pattern of sustained 'hell for leather' racing; but the subsequent running was pedestrian by the standards of the 'ninety-five'. And then, in the small hours of 1 July 1906 came the almost inevitable disaster. It was a disaster all the more significant to the present theme; because the shock of public opinion was such as to slam the door against any future acceleration of train service in Great Britain for many years to come. Although this is taking the London & South Western side of the story two years ahead it is to emphasize the point that despite this apparent recklessness on a very bad piece of line the South Western never rose beyond second place in the 'Race from the West' in 1904.

How the Great Western Railway built up to their Record of Records on 9 May 1904 is a fascinating story; but while the combined efforts of *City of Truro* and *Duke of Connaught* produced the astonishing overall time of 3 hours 46 minutes 48 seconds from Millbay Crossing to Paddington, including a stop of 3min 43sec at Pylle Hill Junction, Bristol, to change engines, and detach the rearmost van which contained the North Country mails, there were certain stretches of line over which even faster running had been made during the building-up period. For example, on 9 May the time over the 19·9 miles uphill from Exeter to Whiteball summit was 19min 29sec; but on 9 April the *City of Exeter*, starting dead from St Davids station, passed Whiteball in 19min 30sec. The speed on passing the summit was exactly 60mph as compared with 52mph by the *City of Truro* on 9 May. Again, on 30 April, the Dean 4-2-2 *Duke of Connaught* is reported by the guard's journal as having run from Pylle Hill Junction to Paddington in 99 minutes, against the 99min 46sec logged by Rous-Marten with the same engine on 9 May. Although the load was one of only two vans on the former occasion the intermediate times taken by the guard were also given as faster, as follows:

PYLLE HILL JUNCTION–PADDINGTON

4-2-2 engine No 3065 *Duke of Connaught*

Date *Load Vans*		*30 April* 2	*9 May* 4
Distance *miles*		*Time* *min*	*Time* *min*
0·0	Pylle Hill Junction	0	0
41·4	Swindon	39	39½
65·6	Didcot	57½	59
82·7	Reading	71	72
118·7	Paddington	99	99¾

Because of the magnificent climb to Whiteball the run made by *City of Exeter* on 9 April must also be included, and no less from the fact that over the 43·7 miles from Taunton to Bedminster the *City of Exeter* beat the *City of Truro* by 53 seconds, making an average speed of 75·8mph, against 74mph. What is more remarkable is that the overall time from Stoke Canon to Bedminster, 71 miles, was 57min 30sec by *City of Exeter* against 59min 25sec by *City of Truro*. The respective average speeds were 74·2 and 71·8mph. It is

Upper: GWR The Gooch 8 ft. single 'Great Britain' which made the Paddington-Didcot record of 1848

Lower: One of the later 8-footers, 'Sultan', but still having no cab, and seat for travelling porter on the tender

LNWR SINGLES

Upper: One of McConnell 'Patent' 2-2-2s

Lower: John Ramsbottom's 'Lady of the Lake' with cab and Webb-style boiler mountings as running at the time of the 1888 race

CELEBRITIES OF THE SCOTTISH RACING

Upper: The Caledonian 4-2-2 No. 123, as originally built

Lower: A Holmes 6 ft. 6 in. 4-4-0 No. 218 of the North British

NORTH EASTERN RACERS
Top: 2-cylinder Class J Compound 4-2-2 No. 1517
Centre: 2-cylinder Class F Compound 4-4-0 No. 779
Bottom: M class 4-4-0 single No. 1638

FAMOUS CALEDONIAN 4-4-0s

Top: The Lambie 4-4-0 No. 17, maker of the Perth-Aberdeen record of 1895

Centre: Drummond 4-4-0 No. 79 'Carbrook'

Bottom: Engine No. 723 of the first Dunalastair class

NORTH WESTERN POWER IN 1895

Top: A Lady of the Lake, No. 44 'Harlequin' as rebuilt in 1895

Centre: 'Hardwicke', the record breaker

Bottom: One of the Teutonic class of 3-cylinder compounds, No. 1302 'Oceanic'

4-4-0S OF THE SOUTHERN LINES

Top: LSWR: an Adams outside cylinder 4-4-0 No. 563

Centre: Ex-LCDR 4-4-0 of M Class in the wartime SECR livery

Bottom: A Brighton B4, No. 43 'Bessborough' in the original yellow livery, and fitted experimentally with Drummond cross-watertubes in the firebox

MIDLAND 'SPINNERS'

Upper: Pioneer engine of the famous 4-2-2 series: engine No. 25 of 1887

Lower: A 7 ft. 9 in. engine of 1896, posed near Millers Dale with a train of the new corridor stock for the Anglo-Scottish expresses. It was No. 117 of this class that attained a speed of 90 m.p.h.

GREAT WESTERN RECORD BREAKERS

Upper: The celebrated 4-2-2 engine No. 3065 'Duke of Connaught'

Lower: 'The City of Bath' decorated for the special run of July 1903, conveying the Prince and Princess of Wales

90 M.P.H.-TYPES: 1900-10

Top: The Midland Johnson compound No. 2632 in original condition

Centre: Great Western Saint class 4-6-0 of which class No. 2915 attained 90 m.p.h.

Bottom: A North Western Experiment, No. 2027 'Queen Empress'

RECORD-MAKING OVER THE YEARS

Top: The pre-1914 fastest train: NER 1.9 p.m. Darlington to York, with superheater R class 4-4-0 No. 1207 at Wiske Moor troughs

Centre: The Cheltenham Flyer at full speed with engine No. 5048, then named 'Barbury Castle'

Bottom: The LMS record-breaker of 1936, the 'Princess Elizabeth', on a heavy Anglo-Scottish express topping Beattock summit

CHURCHWARD DERIVATIVES

Upper: GWR No. 5016 'Montgomery Castle' decorated for working the World's Fastest Train

Lower: Brobdingnagian haulage on the LMS: a Stanier 4-6-2 No. 46206 'Princess Marie Louise' on the Midday Scot

'HE CORONATION PACIFICS
Jpper: The ceremonial emergence of No. 6220 from the Crewe erecting shop
n 1937
ower: The 'City of Birmingham' alongside a replica of the 'Rocket'

GRESLEY RECORD-BREAKERS
Upper: 'Silver Link', as originally built
Lower: 'Mallard', carrying the memorial plaque celebrating the world record speed

CONTRAST IN FAST TRAINS

pper: A Stirling 8-footer, with train of the 1895 period

ower: The Southern 4-6-2 'Clan Line', that attained a speed of 104 m.p.h.

KING RICHARD III: 108 M.P.H.
Upper: The engine as newly out-shopped from Swindon with twin-orific blast pipe and double chimney
Lower: Hauling an up West of England express on the Bruton bank

true that on this journey the *City of Exeter* had come on fresh at Exeter itself; but so far as record-breaking was concerned the traditional disadvantages of a cold start seem to have worked the other way! The exceptional merit of this run, which was logged by the Rev W. J. Scott, seems to have been obscured by subsequent events; but without wishing to debunk the *City of Truro* one cannot gainsay that difference of two minutes in the time between Stoke Canon and Bedminster, whatever happened on 9 May in the descent of Wellington bank.

OCEAN MAIL

9 April 1904
Load: 5 vans, 150 tons full
Engine: 4-4-0 No 3442 *City of Exeter*

Distance miles		*Time m s*	*Av Speed mph*
0·0	EXETER	0 00	—
1·3	*Cowley Bridge Junction*	2 40	—
3·5	Stoke Canon	5 00	56·7
14·9	Tiverton Junction	15 02	68·2
19·9	*Whiteball Box*	19 30	67·2
23·7	Wellington	23 02	64·7
30·8	TAUNTON	27 55	87·1
55·9	*Uphill Junction*	47 24	77·2
74·5	Bedminster	62 30	74·3
75·6	TEMPLE MEADS	65 24	

Before leaving the Bristol and Exeter I should mention another run of great merit. On 30 April the *City of Exeter* was the engine from Plymouth; but having made some exceptionally fast running as far as Newton Abbot, to which detailed reference will be made shortly, she developed a minor defect, and had to come off the train at Exeter. The Dean 4-2-2 No 3052 *Sir Richard Grenville* was commandeered at a moment's notice, and promptly ran the 74·9 miles to Pylle Hill Junction in 68 minutes. Naturally the 'single-wheeler' did not make such a rapid start as the *City of Exeter*, and her time to Taunton was 31min against 27min 55sec; but after that she ran in magnificent style, completing the last 43·9 miles from Taunton to the stop at Pylle Hill in 37 minutes, according to the guard's journal, against 37min 29sec logged by the Rev W. J. Scott with the *City of Exeter*. The 4-2-2 *Sir Richard Grenville* had one coach less; but even so some truly record running must have been involved along the Somersetshire levels, with sustained speeds of 75 to 78mph on the flat. On this account engine No 3052 *Sir Richard Grenville* is fully entitled to participate in the glory won by the Great Western locomotives of 1904 in the working of the Ocean Mails.

The successive speeding up of the running over the South Devon line was one of the phenomena of this particular race. When we bear in mind the exceptional difficulties of the route, as emphasised when discussing the speed of the Royal special of 1903, the following performances are extraordinary:

Date	*Engine*	*Load*	*Times*	
		Vans	*Newton Abbot*	*Exeter*
18/4/04	*City of Exeter*	5	45	68
23/4/04	*City of Exeter*	5	41	66
30/4/04	*City of Exeter*	4	37	60*
2/5/04	*City of Gloucester*	5	37	58
7/5/04	*City of Exeter*	5	40	61
9/5/04	*City of Truro*	5	36¾	59†

* To stop: all other runs passing through at reduced speed
† Includes time lost by permanent way check near Starcross

It is the times between Plymouth and Newton Abbot that make a modern reader's hair stand on end, particularly as they relate to a start from Millbay Crossing, and not from

North Road Station. With two Warships and a load of nine coaches the up Cornish Riviera Express is now allowed 43 minutes to cover the 31·8 miles from North Road to Newton Abbot. From passing North Road at a little under 30mph to passing Newton Abbot the *City of Truro* took 33min 35sec – a breathtaking average, over such a route, of 56·7mph. And this hair-raising performance must have been almost exactly paralleled by the *City of Exeter* on 30 April and by the *City of Gloucester* on 2 May. The latter engine was in the lead for the fastest run ever, as far as Exeter; but it was after passing through that station that the *City of Truro* came prominently into the picture. Even so, if she had run as hard as the *City of Exeter* on 9 April a further two minutes could have been clipped off the overall Plymouth–Bristol record.

Apart from this magnificent non-stop time of 127·8 miles from Millbay Crossing to Pylle Hill Junction in 123min 19sec on 9 May, the most intriguing feature of the run was of course the descent of Wellington bank, where on the basis of a quarter-mile clocked in 8·8 seconds. Rous-Marten claimed a maximum speed of 102·3mph. This claim has in more recent years been the subject of some controversy; but when writing my book *Fifty Years of Western Express Running* in 1954, in commemoration of the fiftieth anniversary of the making of the Ocean Mail record, I sifted through all the evidence, and examined it in the light of recent experience both of actual running and mechanical engineering theory, and I then came to the conclusion that a maximum speed of at least 100mph could be accepted. For those who would wish to follow out the argument that led me to this conclusion I have prepared an appendix, in which the recorded facts and my own interpretation of them are set forth. Apart from the technicalities of the question, one point must be cleared up here. It is the story that the maximum speed remained a secret for several years afterwards. It is true that Rous-Marten was asked – nay implored! – to keep the 102·3 out of the technical press; but on the very next morning the *Western Daily Mercury* had a long and very accurate account of the run, including a twice-repeated statement that the speed had been 'between ninety-nine and a hundred miles an hour'. A special correspondent of that newspaper had, by invitation of the GWR, travelled on the train throughout from Plymouth to Paddington. It is quite evident that all concerned were out to make a record that would last for all time, and intended that it should be amply documented.

The continuation of the run, from Pylle Hill Junction to Paddington, was also a magnificent piece of locomotive performance, seeing that four mail vans of the newest and heaviest type were conveyed. But whether it can be claimed as the pre-1914 Bristol–London record is not clear. The time recorded by Rous-Marten was 99min 46sec, and the time logged in the journal was 100min. This latter was beaten by the *Duke of Connaught* on 30 April when the journal time was recorded as 99min, but with only two coaches. What is beyond any question is the average speed recorded by Rous-Marten over the 70·3 miles from Shrivenham to Westbourne Park, precisely *eighty miles per hour.* This was a record that stood completely unchallenged in British railway history as a piece of long-sustained high-speed running, until the acceleration of the Cheltenham Flyer in 1929. The average over the 34·7 miles from Reading to Westbourne Park was even higher, namely 80·5mph, and over the 17·8 miles between Twyford and West Drayton it was 82·9mph. This was marvellous running for a 4-2-2 engine with so relatively heavy a load as 120 tons. As a postscript to the events of 9 May 1904, it seems that the South Western was completely out of it on that day; the passengers were brought to London by a Great Western special, which left Plymouth, according to the *Western Daily Mercury,* at 9.48am, 25 minutes after the mail, and arrived at Paddington at 2.12pm, a total time of 4hr 24min. But the newspaper gives no other details, except the name of the guard. So far as the mail train was concerned the *Western Daily Mercury* entitled its article 'New and Final GWR Record', and it only remains for me to add that the run of the *Duke of Connaught* from Pylle Hill to Paddington remained the British start-to-stop speed record, at 71·3mph, until the Great Western four-cylinder 4-6-0s brought the Swindon–Paddington run below 65min.

CHAPTER SEVEN

FLASHES IN THE DOLDRUMS

THE ALARMING derailment at Preston on 15 August 1896 of the very train that had been involved in the racing of a year earlier, although not involving very serious loss of life, fairly slammed the door upon further speed enterprise by the East Coast and West Coast Routes to Scotland. Then the exciting Ocean Mail contest, which was continued sporadically by the Great Western and London & South Western Railways for some time after the Record of Records on 9 May 1904, was brought violently to an end by the terrible accident to the South Western American special at Salisbury in the small hours of 1 July 1906. In between the accidents at Preston and Salisbury some fascinating new records were set up, two of them in distinctly unlikely circumstances. Both of these latter were on the London, Brighton & South Coast Railway, a line that hitherto had shown not the slightest inclination to make records, except perhaps at the opposite end of the speed scale.

On 22 January 1901 Queen Victoria died after her lengthy and eventful reign of 64 years. Naturally her funeral was made the occasion of pageantry of the most extensive and solemn kind, and there was probably the greatest gathering of European Royalty ever seen together in history. The Queen died at her home at Osborne, Isle of Wight, and the funeral was arranged to take place at Windsor on 2 February. King Edward VII personally selected the route to be taken by the cortège. The coffin was borne across the Solent in the Royal Yacht on 1 February, and landed at Clarence Yard. Thence on the following morning it was to be conveyed to London. King Edward chose the Brighton route rather than the South Western presumably for the convenience of having a shorter procession across London, to Paddington, though the South Western had the task of conveying the Royal Funeral Train to Fareham, where the direction of running was reversed, and the Brighton took over. The route to Victoria via Chichester, Arundel, Horsham and Dorking is hardly a high-speed route at any time, and one would not expect fast running with a Royal Special, and a funeral cortège at that. The schedule provided 122 minutes for a non-stop run of 87 miles, a reasonable enough average speed, for such an occasion, of 42·8mph. The train consisted of eight coaches, including Queen Victoria's saloon, from the Great Western Railway, which contained the coffin. The tare load was about 190 tons, and probably about 205 tons gross behind the tender.

The passengers included many of the Crowned Heads of Europe including Kaiser Wilhelm II of Germany, and King Edward VII was to meet the train on arrival at Victoria. It was once said that the driver of the train on such an occasion had the destiny of half the world in his hand on the regulator; that a misjudgement on his part could plunge the whole world into mourning. This plain statement makes all the more remarkable the working of the train on that bitterly cold morning of 2 February 1901. There was some delay in leaving Clarence Yard, and the London & South Western Railway brought the special into Fareham eight minutes late. There the time of four minutes allowed for changing engines and testing brakes proved inadequate, and the departure was not until 9.8am, ten minutes late. In the meantime the advance pilot engine, a Billington B4 class 4-4-0 No 53 *Sirdar*, had left ten minutes earlier. On the Royal Train itself another B4 No 54 *Empress* was used, and Mr Billinton himself and J. Richardson, Outdoor Locomotive Superintendent, rode on the footplate. As King Edward's dislike of unpunctuality was well known, the driver, Walter Cooper, was instructed to make up as much of the lateness as he could, and a most remarkable run resulted. On the straight and level stretches of the coastal line between Havant and Ford Junction he attained a maximum speed of 80 mph, and although careful attention was paid to the negotiation of the many junctions, such as Ford, Horsham, Dorking and Mitcham, there was some fast running intermediately, and to everyone's gratification the train arrived in Victoria two minutes early, having averaged 47½mph throughout the 87 miles from Fareham.

By comparison with some of the runs described in earlier chapters of this book this may not seem anything out of the ordinary; but the route was a very difficult one, and while one might take certain risks in a contest such as the 'ninety-five', such might not be taken with such a precious human freight as that conveyed on 2 February 1901. In later years the Brighton railway booked an express non-stop from Clapham Junction to Fratton 81·7 miles in 106 minutes, an average speed of 46·2mph; but in starting from Clapham Junction and terminating at Fratton this regular run had a considerable advantage over the Royal Train in that it avoided slow running in the inner London area and also that over the spur from Cosham to Farlington Junction, which was limited to 20mph for nearly a mile. Not the least appreciative of the fine running made on this solemn occasion was the Kaiser, who, through an equerry, sent his congratulations to the driver and fireman. He considered it was a remarkable performance for a locomotive of such relatively small size as compared with those then running in Germany. So it was, though the German railways were not exactly famed for speed at that moment in history. The attainment of a maximum speed of 80mph on the level, with a load of 205 tons, was certainly a record achievement for a British locomotive in the year 1901. Among some of those who travelled by the train there was a firmly held belief that a maximum speed of 92mph was attained in the descent from Holmwood to Dorking. More recent scrutiny of the facts suggests however that the speed did not greatly exceed

75mph on this particular stretch. What is established beyond question is that the 87 miles from Fareham to Victoria were covered in 110 minutes, instead of the 122 minutes scheduled.

Very early in the new century the neophytes were getting into their stride. Steam was outdated and already on the way out! The promotion of a Bill to construct a high-speed electric railway from London to Brighton was nevertheless taken very seriously by the management of the LB & SCR because for the first time that railway was threatened with competition. It is perhaps not realised to what extent the leisurely timetables and bad timekeeping of the nineteenth century were due to there being no opposition. The London, Brighton & South Coast Railway had an absolute monopoly in much of the territory it served. But the electric railway project promised a non-stop service in 50 minutes between London and Brighton, and their supporters were loud in asserting that the existing railway could not do this. On the past form of the LB&SCR the critics had ample reason for their scepticism. Even if the locomotives had been capable of such running, the traffic working was so inefficient that such fast trains never got a clear road. The management took the challenge very seriously, however, and on Sunday 26 July 1903 a special demonstration was staged. In so doing it was nevertheless admitted frankly enough that the kind of running they proposed could not as yet be done regularly. Extensive alterations and widening of the line had been in progress for some time, to remove the old bottlenecks and chronic causes of delay – these in addition to the Red Hill avoiding line, which had been opened since 1 April 1900. The twentieth-century management of the Brighton railway were anxious to make it plain to all interested parties that the only obstacle in the way of a 60mph average speed between London and Brighton was the difficulty of getting a clear road, owing to the volume of existing traffic. Once the route had been completely modernised they would find no difficulty in equalling the best speed promised by the electric railway promoters, and at infinitely less cost. So the demonstration run was planned and the locomotive department was instructed to get to Brighton as quickly as possible, and certainly in not more than 50 minutes. The load conveyed was 130 tons. The engine chosen was one of the latest B4 class 4-4-0s No 70 *Holyrood,* and as an independent observer was required to provide the subsequent publicity Charles Rous-Marten was invited to travel by the train.

Some remarkable running was made. As with the Royal Funeral train in February 1901, Mr J. J. Richardson rode on the footplate, while Mr Billinton travelled in the train. I always feel that outside the close circle of Brighton enthusiasts the B4 class 4-4-0s, the Scotchmen, as they were familiarly known, have never been awarded the honour they deserved. They had a slender appearance that rather belied their ample proportions, and this run in particular was to confirm both their hill-climbing ability and their speed. In prefacing his account of the two runs, out and home, Rous-Marten went to some length to emphasise the bad rail conditions; but these seemed to have not the slightest effect on the performance. Up the 1 in 264 gradient from East Croydon to Stoats Nest Junction, where the Red Hill avoiding line began, speed was steadily maintained at 62½ to 64mph. Rous-Marten did not quote the actual minimum speeds on the steeper gradients of the new line, leading to the summit point in Quarry Tunnel, but once clear of the North Downs some very fast running developed.

Acceleration was a little restrained at first, down the remaining three miles of the new line, and over the junction at Earlswood, but then on the 1 in 264 descent of the original line speed was work up to 80½mph at Horley, and the 5 subsequent miles at 1 in 264 up to Balcombe Tunnel were cleared at a minimum speed of 66½mph. This was excellent work. Then, down the long and well aligned descent through Haywards Heath to Wivelsfield, an uninterrupted 8½ miles almost entirely at 1 in 264, speed rose until a maximum of 90mph was attained at the foot of the incline. This speed was corroborated by two other independent observers. The target of a 50-minute run was now virtually in the bag. Rous-Marten reported that on the subsequent ascent through Clayton Tunnel, again rising at 1 in 264, the minimum speed was not much below 70, and he attributed the leisurely final approach to Brighton to the slippery condition of the rails. I can, however, scarcely credit that there was any danger of the wheels 'picking up'. The entry to Brighton station was apparently very slow, and caused Rous-Marten to wish they had stopped some distance short of the buffer stops in order to cut the start-to-stop time. This was 48min 41sec, an overall average of 62·7mph. Before evening however the weather had deteriorated considerably, and with a strong cross-wind and the hindrance of some slight permanent way slacks the return journey took 50min 21sec, with the speed not exceeding a maximum of 85mph.

By old time Brighton standards such times and speeds were phenomenal, as well as bringing Mr Billinton's fine B4 class locomotive into the select band of those which, by the year 1903, had attained a maximum speed of 90mph. It only needs to be added, by way of a postscript to the events of 26 July 1903, that the project for an independent electric railway was stillborn, and with the collapse of this threatened opposition the Brighton railway quietly dropped any ideas of a 50-minute service from London. It is only fair to add that the growing number of express trains making the journey in the even hour developed a very high standard of punctuality, and that even with electrification of the Brighton line itself, from 1931, the overall time has not been appreciably reduced. The runs of 26 July 1903 – 48min 41sec down and 50min 21sec – still remain the London–Brighton records today.

At that time there was considerable discussion among students of locomotive performance upon the relative merits of 'single' and 'coupled' engines for very high speed running. The general feeling was that a 'single', being inherently freer running than a coupled engine, should be capable of higher maximum speeds. The homely words of Patrick Stirling, that a coupled engine was like 'a laddie runnin' wi' his breeks doon', were widely accepted, though perhaps in more technical terms. Yet one after another the higher speed records were being made by 4-4-0 and not 4-2-2 locomotives. Apart from the great record of the *City of Truro* Rous-Marten had isolated instances of 96mph by a Johnson Belpaire 4-4-0 on the Midland Railway, and of no less than 97½mph behind a Great Western Atbara. As spot recordings these must be treated with a certain amount of reserve, because the circumstances in which they were attained are not very fully documented. But a record of somewhat greater significance and undoubted authenticity concerns one of the first of the Midland compounds. The two original engines, 2631 and 2632, were at first used entirely between Leeds and Carlisle. They had independent control of the high-pressure and low-pressure valve gear, which in the hands of a skilful driver would permit of much freer running at high speed than the combined gear used on all the later compounds built both for the Midland and for the LMS Railway.

Shortly after the new engines had gone into regular service Rous-Marten travelled behind No 2632 on an up Scottish express from Carlisle. The load was 240 tons and some very fine work was done on the 48·3 mile climb to Aisgill summit. They made, indeed, the almost unprecedented time of 57min 38sec to passing the summit box, an uphill average of 57mph. But then, and obviously for Rous-Marten's benefit, the engine was taken at high speed down from Blea Moor to Settle Junction. A maximum of 92mph was attained and sustained for two miles. This, according to all published data, is the highest authenticated speed ever attained in the long history of the Midland Compounds. In later years when a vast number of runs was logged by many experienced recorders the maximum I have seen was 86mph and this in itself was rather exceptional. The general maximum was around 82 to 83mph. It might seem strange that this early record taken by Rous-Marten should not have been surpassed when so much attention was given to the design and working of these engines, and when track conditions were better and modern rolling stock had a lower rolling resistance. Furthermore engine No 2632 was not superheated at the time of her 92mph sprint down from Blea Moor.

I have mentioned earlier the change in the valve gear controls. All the compounds except Nos 2631 and 2632 had an arrangement whereby the gear for both high- and low-pressure cylinders was linked up simultaneously. It is sometimes thought that this change was made by Johnson's successor, R. M. Deeley, as a means of simplifying the technique of driving. Deeley certainly changed the design of the regulator, but it was Johnson himself who put the combined reverser gear on to the three compounds that he built in 1903, namely Nos 2633–5. This arrangement unfortunately had the effect of altering the volume ratios between the high- and low-pressure systems as the engine was linked up, and introduced such a degree of throttling in the low pressure as to impose a virtual limit on maximum speed, especially if an engine was being driven hard. On the Midland Railway with its strict limitation of loads this did not matter, because the powerful compounds could climb the gradients at such a speed as to make very fast running downhill unnecessary. With engines 2631 and 2632 in their original condition the low-pressure cylinders could be left working in a fairly long cut-off, with good valve openings for admission, and exhaust. There would be no throttling effect, and the locomotives could and did, attain much higher maximum speeds.

I remember having a most interesting discussion many years later with a particularly keen and intelligent LMS express driver stationed at Wakefield (L & Y section). In the course of his work he drove both two- and three-cylinder Stanier 4-6-0s, Midland compounds, and the LMS standard Class '2' 4-4-0s, which had long travel valves. The compounds were great favourites of his, though I shall always remember him saying that he wished they had independent cut-off 'like the French do', as he put it. 'They could run much faster like that,' he added. It would have been very interesting to see how the two original Johnson compounds would have performed with superheated steam; they were actually among the very first compounds to be superheated, but at the time of their conversion they had the standard form of combined reversing gear. So Rous-Marten's record with No 2632 – afterwards No 1001 – remained the record for the whole class.

The performance of the *City of Truro* in 1904 went some way towards exploding the old theory that one must have a single-wheeler to do exceptionally high speeds. Before his untimely death in 1908 Rous-Marten was to witness what could be done with a six-coupled engine, and moreover one having coupled wheels no larger than 6ft 3in in diameter. In many ways the Experiment class 4-6-0s of the London & North Western Railway provide one of the greatest puzzles of locomotive history. They followed the introduction of the celebrated Precursors of 1904; but with large numbers of the latter engines already at work in 1905 there was not the same shipwreck hurry to get quantity production of the Experiments, and their introduction on the Crewe–Carlisle section was more gradual. Although some difficulty was at first experienced in firing a grate of a design new to the North Western, resulting in spells of indifferent steaming, the new engines proved extremely free-running – and most surprisingly so. On his first run with the pioneer engine, No 66 *Experiment*, Rous-Marten clocked a sustained maximum speed of 93¾mph on the falling gradients between Penrith and Carlisle. Although so high a maximum was not clocked again with any of the class several instances of speeds of the same order were recorded by other observers. Rous-Marten's stop-watching activities came to an end with his sudden death in 1908, and henceforth for a period of some twenty years it is the writings of R. E. Charlewood, Cecil J. Allen and the Rev W. J. Scott that provide running data concerning British locomotive performance.

The speedworthiness of the Experiments was confirmed on two particular occasions in the travels of Cecil J. Allen. Engine No 887 *Fortuna* gave him a maximum speed of 86½mph in the same locality in which Rous-Marten clocked 93¾mph with *Experiment*, and then on the southbound descent from Shap No 830 *Phosphorus* piloted by a 2-4-0 'Jumbo' momentarily touched 90mph before Tebay. It could be argued that the pilot was contributing in no small measure to the attainment of this high speed; but on the contrary, if either engine of the combination had been in any way constrained such a high speed would not have been possible. We know that the Jumbos were extremely fast engines, and the Experiments likewise, on the unassisted showings of *Experiment* herself and *Fortuna*. The fact certainly remains that these most unlikely engines, non-superheated, with relatively small six-coupled wheels, were the *only* LNWR locomotives ever to be authentically recorded at over 90mph. The front-end layout must have been particularly propitious, because their superheated successors of the Prince of Wales class, with piston valves instead of slide valves, never showed any ability towards free running at speeds in excess of 80mph. In all other respects, of course, they were incomparably better engines than the Experiments.

With the solitary exception of the Great Western outside-framed, inside-cylindered 4-4-0s there seemed a general ceiling of maximum speed achievement in Great Britain of around 90 to 93mph. On the Great Western Churchward's new 4-6-0s had such a vast reserve of power that very high downhill speeds were unnecessary. The target for optimum performance had been set by Churchward himself at 70mph. But both the two-cylinder Saint class and the four-cylinder Stars had in their valve gear and excellent layout of steam-ports, passages and exhaust arrangements all the ingredients of a very free-running engine, and it was with one of the Saints that Cecil J. Allen recorded his first example of sustained running at 90mph. The Jumbo and Experiment feat, at the foot of Shap, was no more than momentary.

With the opening of the shortened route from Paddington to Birmingham, via Bicester, and the inauguration of a two-hour service in competition with the London & North Western Railway the loads conveyed on the majority of trains were not heavy, and on most of those that included an intermediate stop a concession was made, providing an extra five minutes in the overall time. Completely uninhibited high speed was at first not desirable over the entirely new section of the route between Ashendon and Aynho Junctions, and if really fast running was needed to make up lost time elsewhere it had to be made on the older and fully consolidated stretches. Cecil J. Allen had a remarkable instance of this on the 2.45pm up express from Birmingham, with engine No 2915 *Saint Bartholomew*, hauling a load of 320 tons. There had been various speed restrictions on the new line, and the engine was afterwards given her head down the long and favourably aligned descent from Beaconsfield to the outskirts of London. At the foot of the steepest part of the descent, the stretch between Gerrards Cross and Denham, Allen clocked three alternate quarter miles in exactly 10 seconds each, representing a maximum of 90mph sustained for at least 1¼ miles. The average over the 13 miles from Gerrards Cross to Park Royal was exactly 80mph.

When war came in August 1914, and with it a general slowing down of train services, two 4-6-0 designs had thus joined the select ranks of the 90mph and over 'club'; but it was not for many years afterwards that such high speeds were again to be noted, even occasionally, on British metals. The war did however bring one speed record of a remarkable and poignant kind, having regard to its tragic aftermath. In June 1916, only a week after the news of the heavy naval losses in the Battle of Jutland, the whole Empire and all the Allied nations were appalled to learn of the sinking of HMS *Hampshire*, which, in conditions of the greatest secrecy, was conveying Lord Kitchener on a mission to Russia. He and his staff were all drowned. But it is with the prelude to that fateful journey that I am concerned here. A special train conveying Lord Kitchener and his suite left Kings Cross at 5.45pm on Sunday evening, 4 June 1916. It consisted of four coaches, and was drawn by the small-boilered Atlantic engine No 252. No exceptional speed was called for, and this light train was run at the normal speed of the prewar Flying Scotsman. Before the special was half an hour on its way however a representative of the Foreign Office arrived at Kings Cross with important documents and stated that he must catch the Kitchener special. A second train was therefore organised at very short notice. When the first train stopped at Grantham to change engines Lord Kitchener was advised by telephone of what had happened, and it was arranged that the first special should wait at York for the arrival of the second.

It was obviously essential to run the second train at the maximum speed possible in the circumstances. It was the *Trent* case all over again: a matter of conveying urgent dispatches – though on 4 June 1916 things had to be organised at a moment's notice. Two coaches only were needed, and the first main line engine and crew available were put on to the job. The engine was the Royal Atlantic No 1442, not from choice, but because she was standing pilot at Kings Cross that evening. They got away at 6.56pm little more than half an hour after the request for a second special was made, and the operating authorities saw to it that they had a wonderfully clear road, at any rate while they were on the Great Northern Railway. In these dramatic circumstances there began the fastest run *ever recorded* between Kings Cross and Doncaster – races of 1888 and 1895 included! It is astonishing to set side by side the logs of the run made on the last night of the 'ninety-five' and that of the second Kitchener special (see page 122).

It will be seen that the Kitchener special, by running the 58·7 miles from Hatfield to Peterborough in 50 minutes, averaged 70·3mph, against the sedate 67·1mph of the racer of 1895.

At Grantham engines were changed, and superheater

Date	*21/8/95*	*4/6/16*
Engine No	*668*	*1442*
Load: tons	*101*	*70*
Distance miles	*Time min*	*Time min*
0·0 Kings Cross	0	0
17·7 Hatfield	19½	20
31·9 Hitchin	33	32
44·1 Sandy	42¾	42
58·9 Huntingdon	55½	55
76·4 Peterborough	72	70
105·5 Grantham	101	101*

* 4 minutes lost by permanent-way slack

4-4-0 No 57 replaced the Atlantic No 1442. Naturally there had been a little time for preparation at Grantham, and when the fresh engine got away it was to make a remarkable effort. This again makes an interesting comparison with the last night of the 'ninety-five'.

Engine No	*775*	*57*
Distance miles	*Time min*	*Time min*
0·0 Grantham	0	0
14·6 Newark	14	14
33·1 Retford	30½	30
50·5 Doncaster	46	45
54·7 Shaftholme Junction	—	49
68·9 Selby	62 pass	sig checks 63 stop

From Shaftholme Junction onwards the train was subjected to signal checks, and the stop at Selby lasted for five minutes. When they did get away, on account of further checks, the last 13·8 miles from Selby to York took as much as 29 minutes. The delays were estimated to cost about 18 minutes, but despite this the second special arrived at York only 43 minutes after the first. As far as Doncaster, however, the time was the fastest ever, beating the Great Northern record in the 'ninety-five' by a full two minutes thus:

	1895	*1916*
Kings Cross dep	0	0
Grantham arr	101	101
Grantham dep	105	104
Doncaster pass	151	149

The net time in 1916 was 145 minutes, and the running time of 142 minutes gives the notable net average speed of 66·2mph against the best racing average for the same distance of 63·7mph. It is sad to recall that the special envoy who was conveyed from London to York in brilliant style by the Great Northern Railway duly sailed in the *Hampshire*, and perished with Lord Kitchener and the rest of his suite.

CHAPTER EIGHT

UPSURGE ON THE GWR

WHEN THE timetables of the British railways had been reconstructed after the drastic deceleration enforced during the war years the order of priority in the list of fastest start-to-stop runs at first remained much the same as in pre-war years, with the North Eastern heading the list, with its 43-minute run from Darlington to York, and the Great Central bracketed first, with the 22-minute sprint of the early morning newspaper train from Leicester to Arkwright Street, Nottingham. Both trains gave a start-to-stop average speed of 61·5mph. The Great Western came third, and then only by way of slip-coach arrivals at Bath, in 105 minutes from Paddington. The main train in each case made a 59·2mph run, start to stop, from Paddington to Bristol. Before we pass on to the main subject of this chapter however a word is necessary about the North Eastern and Great Central achievements in the way of high speed. For many years the North Eastern had the field to themselves, and the 43-minute run was made by what might have been called a 'freak' train, the 1.9pm from Darlington to York. This was the 10.35am from Alnmouth, a four-coach non-corridor train, that stopped at all stations to Newcastle. There it attached two Midland through coaches for the south, and went forward at 12.20pm, now as an express passenger train, for Sheffield. If the NER wished for show purposes to have the fastest train in the British Isles it was an ideal one for the purpose, for its gross load did not exceed around 170 tons. Sometimes, with one less coach from Alnmouth, it was even less.

When the 43-minute schedule was restored in the summer of 1922 it was applied to what might be termed a much more logical commercial proposition, namely the evening Glasgow–Leeds dining-car express leaving Darlington at 8.49pm. This was a considerably heavier train, composed entirely of modern corridor stock, and weighing between 220 and 300 tons, according to traffic requirements. On the other hand, whereas the pre-war 12.20pm from Newcastle usually had a 4-4-0 of the R class from Gateshead shed, the post-war 8.49pm from Darlington had almost invariably a three-cylinder Atlantic of Class Z. During both phases of its existence the 43-minute schedule was treated as a prestige job, and some very fine running was made. The pre-war record was held by a non-superheated R class 4-4-0 locomotive, No 1672, when with a six-coach train of 170 tons the 44·1 miles from Darlington to York were covered in 39min 34sec, an average speed of 66·9mph. This run was logged by the late R. J. Purves, who eventually became Assistant Signal Engineer of the North Eastern Region of British Railways. In those days, when I came to know him well, he never lost his enthusiasm for recording train speeds; but before World War I he combined with this aspect of his railway interests great skill as a photographer of trains in motion. His acquaintance with many of the drivers resulted as much in spectacular smoke effects when he was at the lineside with his camera as in fast runs when he was travelling in the trains. The fine run of No 1672 from Darlington to York was, like many of Rous-Marten's finest runs, not unconnected with his presence in the train!

On this journey the maximum speed on level track was 77½mph; but before war conditions had led to the abandonment of the schedule Cecil J. Allen had logged a run with a superheated engine of the R class, on which a maximum speed of 80½mph was sustained for five miles continuously, south of Tollerton. The load on that occasion was however one of only five coaches, and light ones at that, totalling no more than 135 tons behind the tender. Nevertheless, bearing in mind the speeds sustained by the Great Western 4-4-0 locomotives on level track, with loads of this order, the work of the North Eastern 4-4-0 No 1207 was certainly significant. In post-war years the Glasgow–Leeds 'diner' had a path when occupation of the line was quite intense, and a clear road was not always obtained. Drivers were inclined to go easily as far as Northallerton, and some very fast running often ensued. One of the finest, logged again by R. J. Purves, was made by Z class three-cylinder Atlantic No 2163, with a load of 220 tons. The start was easy, taking 16¼ minutes to pass Northallerton, 14·1 miles; but the speed had risen to 75mph by Thirsk, and an average of 80·3mph was sustained over the 14·9 miles from Sessay to Skelton Bridge. The maximum was 81¾mph. Because of the easy start, and on account of a slight signal check at the finish, the overall time was only five seconds inside the 43-minute schedule. But such running, on dead level track, was enough to excite the admiration of the most experienced of train-speed recorders.

By the time of the grouping of the railways in 1923, the number of enthusiasts who were becoming expert in the recording of train speeds was growing, and among these was a young locomotive engineer, the late E. L. Diamond, who was at one time a pupil of Sir Henry Fowler on the Midland Railway at Derby, and who later joined the staff of the Institution of Mechanical Engineers. In his younger days Diamond's enthusiasm knew no bounds. Several times he travelled in the one passenger coach attached to the 2.32am Newspaper express from Marylebone, which had three successive start-to-stop runs at around 60mph. It was through his enthusiasm that the first recorded instance of a maximum speed of 90mph on the Great Central line was published. One of the later Director class 4-4-0s, No 501 *Mons*, was on the job with a load of 175 tons, and in gaining a mere 20 seconds on the sharp allowance of 24 minutes, start to stop, over the 23·9 miles from Brackley to Rugby a maximum of 90mph was attained and sustained descending from Catesby Tunnel to Braunston. No higher speed than 85mph was needed however down Whetstone bank to make a gain of a full minute from Rugby to Leicester: 19·9 miles in 18min 55sec. At Leicester, as usual, engines were changed, and an Atlantic No 360 came on to a reduced load of 150 tons for the 61·5mph run on to Arkwright Street. She also went like the wind, completing the run in 21¼ minutes, with maximum speeds of 85mph at Loughborough, and 86½mph at Ruddington. Such were some of the daily feats achieved on the fast schedules of the North Eastern and Great Central Railways. It should be noted however that the Great Central high speed records were attained downhill, and not on level track.

In the summer timetable of 1923 the Great Western Railway booked the 2.30pm up express from Cheltenham to run the 77·3 miles from Swindon to Paddington in 75 minutes, start to stop, and with this average speed of 61·8mph, it captured, by a few decimal points, the distinction of making the fastest run in the British Isles. It was, of course, a relatively easy run from the locomotive point of view, on slightly falling and level track throughout, with a complete absence of speed restrictions, and made at a time of day when the line was fairly clear. The load varied between eight and nine coaches, and for some little time after its inauguration the train was worked by the two-cylinder 4-6-0 No 2915 *Saint Bartholomew*. It is interesting to note in passing that a Saint rather than a four-cylinder Star class 4-6-0 should have been allocated to this important duty; by a coincidence it was the same engine that in pre-war days had given Cecil J. Allen his first instance of a sustained maximum speed of 90mph. On the first day of the new service the train was three minutes early on arrival at Paddington, and when Cecil J. Allen travelled shortly afterwards he logged a time of 73min 55sec, start to stop, despite two permanent-way slacks. He was moved to comment thus:

> Under 70 minutes net for a journey of 77.3 miles, and a slow finish to avoid too early an arrival! If the Great

Western Railway is setting out seriously to capture and retain the blue riband of start-to-stop railway speed, as I remarked previously, in such circumstances as these it would seem idle for any other aspirant so much as to attempt to compete!

These were strong words coming from a man in the service of the newly created London & North Eastern Railway, in which company an engineer by the name of Herbert Nigel Gresley had been appointed Chief Mechanical Engineer. For many years however Allen's prophecy remained entirely correct, though because of the industrial unrest of the later nineteen-twenties the tremendous upsurge was several years in coming. Until the summer of 1929 the order of priority had remained the same, with the 2.30pm up Cheltenham Spa Express leading the same North Eastern and Great Central runs, and the North Western section of the LMS making a good fourth with some 59·2mph runs in each direction over the 107·5 miles between Willesden Junction and Birmingham. In the summer of 1929 however the Great Western cut five minutes out of the Swindon–Paddington schedule, and immediately shot the start-to-stop average up to 66·3mph. This was in many ways a 'paper' acceleration, for it merely confirmed, in a mild way, the kind of running that had frequently been made on the train itself in ordinary service, when delays had to be recovered or the drivers felt like having a go. Before we come to the Cheltenham Flyer, as the train was justifiably becoming known, some isolated but significant speed achievements in other directions must be noted.

By the year 1923 the 90 and over 'club' had been joined by the Great Central Director class 4-4-0s and within the next few years several other well-known classes had entered this select band. First of all, and perhaps the least unexpected, were the Great Western Star class 4-6-0s. During the work of the Bridge Stress Committee Great Western 4-6-0s of both Saint and Star classes were run at high speed, light engine, over the viaduct across the River Parrett, near Langport. The target in both cases was 90mph; but whereas the Saint did not exceed 86mph the Star crossed the bridge at 92mph. This feat, though interesting in itself, does not really qualify for inclusion among the records chronicled in this book, except that it was paralleled not long afterwards by a magnificent piece of running with a revenue-earning train. But before leaving the Bridge Stress Committee I must mention that one of the North Eastern Z class Atlantics obliged with a maximum of 92mph – again light-engine – for the edification of the Committee. The Star performance took place strangely enough during the period of restricted service following the General Strike of 1926, and was a maximum of 92mph by engine No 4067 *Tintern Abbey* down the Fosse Road bank between Southam Road and Leamington. Earlier in the run the same engine had attained a maximum of 90mph in descending from Princes Risborough to Haddenham. The second entrant to the 'club' was the ex-LSWR 4-6-0 No 747, then assimilated to the King Arthur class and named *Elaine*, which gave Cecil J. Allen a 'ninety' descending from Honiton Tunnel to Seaton Junction. Right up to the end of the nineteen twenties however 'nineties' were rare.

And now for the Cheltenham Flyer! Until the acceleration of 1929 the fastest run on record stood to the credit of a Star, No 4059 *Princess Patricia*, whose driver, leaving Swindon 4¾ minutes late, went for it hard to reach Paddington 4 minutes early, on the old 75-minute schedule. The overall time was 66min 12sec, a start-to-stop average speed of 70·2mph. Over the 67·2 miles from Uffington to Acton speed averaged 75mph. This was a remarkably steady performance as the maximum speed did not at any point exceed 82mph. The load was one of 235 tons. This splendid run took place as early as 1924. At that time however there were very few Castles available for anything except the crack West of England workings, and the Bristol top-link duties were still almost entirely in the hands of two-cylinder Saint class. One of these engines – one of the oldest of them all, No 2998 *Ernest Cunard* – was so delayed on the 12.15pm up two-hour Bristol express as to pass Swindon eleven minutes late. This left only 63½ minutes for the remaining 77·3 miles if Paddington was to be reached on time; but with an eight-coach train of about 270 tons gross behind the tender those 77·3 miles were covered in 62 minutes, pass to stop, an amazing average, for that period, of 74·8mph.

The acceleration of 1929 naturally created intense interest among that growing section of railway enthusiasts who took pleasure in the detailed recording and study of train speeds. Mr J. Pattison Pearson, himself the author of several notable railway books, made no less than twenty-seven journeys in the summer of 1929 specially to travel on the Flyer. Things were made easier for some of us by the issue of special half-day excursion tickets from Paddington to Swindon at 5s each, outwards by the 1.18pm and back by the Cheltenham Flyer. Mr Pearson made an analysis of his journeys, selecting the fastest times made over each station-to-station distance, and this, giving the remarkable minimum aggregate of 60min 55sec from Swindon to Paddington, showed that the locomotives had an ample margin in reserve. What was nevertheless extraordinary was that the aggregate fastest times of these twenty-seven runs gave a time over 70·3 miles from Shrivenham to Westbourne Park only 65 seconds faster than that of the *Duke of Connaught* on the Ocean Mail record run of 9 May 1904. If indeed one takes into account the very fast finishing time on the latter run, the inward times from Shrivenham to the stop in Paddington were 53min 59sec on Mr Pearson's aggregate, and 54min 27sec by the *Duke of Connaught*. From Mr Pearson's analysis it would seem that the maximum speeds on level track were around 86 to 87mph. The four-cylinder 4-6-0 locomotives figure exclusively in his records, mostly Castles; but it is nevertheless significant of what lay in reserve that the fastest individual time to passing Ealing Broadway, 71·6 miles from the start, was made by a Star, No 4017 *Knight of*

Liege, in 56min 51sec and only 1min 39sec longer than the fastest aggregate for the whole series.

This engine also made the longest continuous running at an average of 80mph, covering the 60·8 miles from Uffington to Ealing in 45min 14sec, at an actual average of 80·7mph. This was a magnificent achievement, with a load of 239 tons, but, astonishing to relate, it beat by no more than *four seconds* the performance of the *Duke of Connaught* in 1904 over this same stretch. In the autumn of 1929 I made my first journey on the Cheltenham Flyer, and was rewarded by a run on which the fastest aggregate times in Mr Pearson's analysis were beaten by 18 seconds between Didcot and Tilehurst. The engine was No 5003 *Lulworth Castle* and with a gross load of 275 tons behind the tender she averaged 84·5mph from Steventon to Reading with a sustained maximum of 86½mph on level track. Although it seemed evident from a run like this that the Castles had a good deal in reserve if the Great Western Railway had seriously in mind still better speed records with lighter loads, the period of the 70-minute schedule of the Cheltenham Flyer must not be passed over without mention of two other magnificent runs with the older 4-6-0 engines, both with eight-coach trains.

A Star, No 4072 *Tresco Abbey*, made what is believed to be the fastest end-to-end time until the autumn of 1931, namely 64min 24sec, or a net time of 63½ minutes, including two slight delays. The maximum speed did not exceed 83½mph and the good end-to-end time was mainly achieved by an extremely vigorous start out of Swindon. The second run is to my knowledge the only recorded instance of a Saint on the job during the period of the 70-minute schedule. When I say the 'only instance' it should be understood that it is the only instance of which a detailed record has been published. On this occasion, with engine No 2917 *Saint Bernard* and a 260-ton train, the departure from Swindon was 13 minutes late, and although the running was not quite up to the best Star or Castle standards, an end-to-end time of

65min 20sec was achieved, without exceeding 80mph anywhere. This engine made a start out of Swindon that was fractionally faster even than that of *Tresco Abbey*, and before she was checked by signal had covered the 61·1 miles to Langley in 49 minutes 44 seconds from the start. The net time on this excellent run was 64½ minutes, the fastest on record with a Saint class engine.

In 1931 the Blue Riband of world railway speed passed temporarily from the Great Western Railway to the Canadian Pacific, of all railways! One normally associated the CPR with hard slogging up the fearsome gradients in the Rocky Mountains: but there was strong competition between the Canadian Pacific and the Canadian National for the Inter-City traffic between Montreal and Toronto, and the CPR scheduled one express to cover the 124 miles between Smith's Falls and Montreal West in 108 minutes, and a second, in the reverse direction, in 110 minutes. Both these trains, with start-to-stop average speeds of 68·9 and 67·6mph, beat the 66·3mph of the Cheltenham Flyer; but the Great Western did not allow this supremacy to last for long, because on 14 September 1931 three minutes were cut from the Swindon–Paddington timing, bringing the average speed up to 69·2mph. From that date onwards the engine carried a special headboard with the legend 'World's Fastest Train'; and so it certainly was on the basis of booked start-to-stop average speed. But the Great Western were not content with this; on the first three days of the new service the drivers were definitely encouraged to make exceptionally fast runs, just to show, as it were, how much was in reserve. The fact that three different crews were concerned added to the spice of competition, enhanced by the presence of Chief Locomotive Inspector Robinson on the footplate each day.

There was another world record at stake in addition to that of booked average speed. Among the most experienced students and recorders of locomotive performance the fastest-ever start-to-stop run was then considered to have been the one made in May 1905 on one of the Atlantic City Flyers of the Reading Railroad in the USA, which in pre-war years had been scheduled to cover the 55½ miles from Camden, Philadelphia, to Atlantic City, in 50 minutes – a start-to stop average of 66·6mph. On one occasion a time of 42min 33sec was recorded, giving an average of 78·3mph, and the existence of this old record, as yet unbeaten, was not unknown when the Cheltenham Flyer set out on the first run to its accelerated timing on 14 September. The bare results of the first three days running, on each occasion with engine No 5000 *Launceston Castle*, were as follows. On the 14th and 16th the runs were expertly logged in detail; on the 15th only the guard's journal times are available:

THE CHELTENHAM FLYER

September 1931

Date	*14 Sept*	*15 Sept*	*16 Sept*
Driver *Fireman*	*J. W. Street* *F. W. Sherer*	*C. Wasley* *A. Hoyle*	*H. Jones* *C. E. Brown*
Load: tons gross Time Av Speed: mph	190 59m 36s 77·8	230 58min 80¼*	195 58m 20s 80·0

* By guard's journal time

So, on 16 September 1931, the world record for a start-to-stop run passed to the Great Western Railway, with an average speed of exactly 80mph.

Examination of the detailed logs of the first and third of these runs show also that for the first time in history a speed of 90mph was attained, virtually on level track, albeit with no more than a six-coach train of just under 200 tons. On the first day the maximum did not exceed 86¾mph on the gradual descent through the Vale of the White Horse, but reached 89mph between Ealing Broadway and Acton, in the last dash for Paddington. On the third day 90mph was reached at Steventon, and 88mph at Maidenhead. These runs created no small sensation at the time, certain commentators apparently deriving great satisfaction from the fact that the Ocean Mail record was at last beaten. But to see these runs in their proper perspective it is interesting to compare the speeds with the loads hauled and the nominal tractive efforts of the locomotives concerned. In the following table the weight of the tender has been included with the train to give strict comparison of the loads being hauled.

Year	*Railway*	*Route*	*Av Speed mph*	*Engine No*	*Ratios of Weight*	
					Train to Engine	*Train to TE of Engine*
1895	NER	Newcastle–Edinburgh	66·1	1620	2·8	18·2
1895	LNWR	Crewe–Carlisle	67·2	790	2·98	19·4
1904	GWR	Exeter–Bristol*	69·5	3440	3·34	23·2
1904	GWR	Swindon–Paddington*	77·2	3065	3·19	21·9
1931	GWR	Swindon–Paddington	80·0	5000	2·94	16·6

* Pass to stop

In the foregoing table the times of *City of Truro* and *Duke of Connaught* have been taken from the passing times, although in the latter case the existence of a slowing to a walking pace over the bridge over the Cricklade Road just east of Swindon station made the time of 1904 5min 42sec from Swindon to Shrivenham, as compared with 6min 15sec on the world record run on 1931. It will be seen, nevertheless, that *Launceston Castle* both in respect of train weight and locomotive tractive effort had the lightest task of any; and although the record of the *Duke of Connaught* was beaten it was by a relatively narrow margin when the power and weight of the locomotives are taken into consideration. It is very important to appreciate however that although the Great Western Railway was out, unblushingly, to break world records in 1931, the locomotives themselves were not forced. There was no parallel instance to some of the earlier records set out in this book when Rous-Marten or some other enthusiast was at the driver's elbow, as it were, urging him to get the last ounce out of the engine – as Ahrons undoubtedly did when he secured a maximum of 81¾mph with a broad gauge eight-footer descending the Wellington Bank. In 1931 the Great Western Castles were driven at their economic best. On 14 September, for example, No 5000 was worked in 15 per cent cut-off throughout, and the regulator was for the most part some way below the full open position. It could be true that lengthening of the cut-off or using a wider regulator opening could have slowed the engine down, by putting more steam through the cylinders than could be exhausted freely. That is nevertheless an academic point. A world record had been secured by the Great Western Railway.

The year 1931 ended with the supremacy of the Great Western completely unchallenged in Great Britain. The times were hardly propitious for keen industrial enterprise, with the country as a whole in the midst of one of the most serious trade depressions this century. But in 1932 it was soon evident that things were stirring elsewhere. The outcome of these stirrings had scarcely become apparent before the Great Western sought to force its advantage still further home by a remarkable demonstration on 5 June 1932. On that day the most comprehensive preparations were made to set up a new Record of Records, not only running the Cheltenham Flyer at a speed faster than ever before, but also by stopping the corresponding down express specially at Swindon in record time to refute the oft-quoted charge that the fast schedule of the up trains was only possible because the route was all downhill. On that one memorable afternoon engine No 5006 *Tregenna Castle* lowered the record for the up journey to 56min 47sec, while engine No 5005 *Manorbier Castle* hauled a train of 210 tons from Paddington to Swindon, against the very slight gradient, in 60min 1sec. The world record for a start-to-stop run was thus pushed up to 81·68mph, and this still remains the British record with steam traction.

The engine concerned, *Tregenna Castle*, also made a new record, by being the first British steam locomotive to exceed 90mph on a level road. In the previous autumn *Launceston Castle* had reached a maximum speed of 90mph, and this had occurred between Didcot and Steventon, on a falling gradient of 1 in 154. *Tregenna Castle* was no more than slightly exceeding this, up to Didcot; but then, a very slight increase in cut-off by no more than 1 per cent produced an average speed of 90.3mph and a twice repeated maximum of 92 over the 14.5 miles between Didcot and Tilehurst. The maximum was attained down 1 in 1,508 past Cholsey; it fell away to a dead 90 on the level from Goring to Pangbourne, and then increased to 92mph again down 1 in 1,320 to Tilehurst. Reading was passed at 91mph but after that the speed lay between 81½ and 89mph onwards to Ealing Broadway. The average speed over the 70.3 miles from Shrivenham to Westbourne Park was 87.2mph, while over the 29.4 miles from Wantage Road to Twyford it was 90.8mph. This was record breaking with a vengeance. It only remains to add that the schedule time of the Cheltenham Flyer was afterwards cut to 65 minutes, thus pushing up the booked start-to-stop average speed to 71·3mph.

This book is primarily connected with speed records, rather than the commercial or political background to their achievement; and as speed records, both the booked schedule speed of 71·3mph and the great run of 6 June 1932 stood unchallenged at the time in British railway history. Those with partisan feelings elsewhere however dismissed the Cheltenham Flyer as a stunt train, and one, moreover, by which commercial interests were apt to be disdained. There was a local train calling at all stations up from Bath which was most annoyingly timed to arrive at Swindon three minutes after the Flyer was due to depart. This arrangement I well remember, because it was of some concern to the management of Westinghouse Brake and Signal Company. There were many occasions when important visitors were welcomed at the Chippenham Works, frequently from overseas railways; how better to end their day than to give them a trip back to London on the World's Fastest Train! But it couldn't be done, because of that wretched three minutes' lack of connection at Swindon. More than once representations were made in the highest quarters at Paddington, only to receive some highly 'technical' operating reason why that sluggard of a local could not be speeded up enough to make the connection!

Although it is carrying the story forward five years, and well out of chronological order with the speed achievements secured by the northern lines in the years 1932–7, one more run of the Cheltenham Flyer must be mentioned. In 1937 the Great Western Railway was engaged in fitting speed indicators on locomotives of the Castle and King classes. This of course was to ensure the accurate observance of speed limits where they were enforced; but needless to say their installation tempted some of the more enterprising drivers to see what their engines could do on the open road. Four circumstances combined to provide a run of unusual interest on 30 June 1937. The engine booked for the Cheltenham Flyer, No 5039 *Rhuddlan Castle*, had recently been fitted with a speed indicator; a young engineer from Swindon was deputed to ride on the footplate for observation purposes; the previous day the LMS, with the new Coronation Scot train, had made a run from Crewe to Euston that came very near to thc Great Western start-to-stop world record; and finally a driver of rare enterprise and skill, F. W. Street, was at the regulator. This driver decided to have a go, and fortunately an experienced recorder of train speeds, the Rev

J. H. Phillips, was a passenger. The load was one coach heavier than on the Record of Records, scaling 235 tons gross behind the tender.

The start out of Swindon was slightly slower, but *Rhuddlan Castle* was doing 90mph no farther from Swindon that Uffington, 10.8 miles, and she then proceeded to average 91.8mph over the ensuing 21.8 miles on to Goring. At Steventon the maximum was 95mph and on passing Goring they were absolutely level with *Tregenna Castle* despite the slower start. After falling back very slightly after Reading, *Rhuddlan Castle* went ahead again with some very fast running, and a maximum of 93mph was attained at Maidenhead. Indeed, over the 62·5 miles from Shrivenham to Southall the average speeds were 88·0mph by *Tregenna Castle* and 88·9 by *Rhuddlan Castle*. At Southall the latter engine, despite the slower start and the extra coach, was 5 seconds ahead of the Record of Records! But the train was then nearly six minutes early, and having tested the speedometer the engine was eased right down and arrived only four minutes early, in 61min 7sec from Swindon. Even so, the average speed from Shrivenham to Westbourne Park was 83mph and for just over 50 miles – 50·3 to be exact – from Uffington to Langley, the average speed was 90·3mph. Although not improving upon the Record of Records, so far as end-to-end time was concerned *Rhuddlan Castle* made two new records for the GWR: the maximum speed for the Cheltenham Flyer run of 95mph, and the longest continuous stretch yet done at 90mph. Had the Rev J. H. Phillips been logging every milepost, as was done with *Tregenna Castle* in June 1932, it is likely that the continuous stretch at over 90mph might have been longer. But the section from Uffington to Langley is the longest station to station distance to show an average of 90mph.

CHAPTER NINE

GRESLEY METEORITES

EVER SINCE the end of the Cockshott era the Great Northern Railway had played a minor, nay insignificant, part in the development of British railway passenger-train speeds. This situation continued through the early grouping years. Gresley had no delusions about the shortcomings of his first Pacifics, in comparison with the performance of the Ivatt large-boilered Atlantics which he had so brilliantly modernised; and he had accepted the challenge of the 1925 Interchange Trials with the Great Western with considerable reluctance. The publicity that followed the conclusion of those trials was distasteful to railwaymen of all ranks, wherever their partisan feelings might lie. It went immeasurably deeper with Gresley; and those closest to him knew how he looked forward to opportunities to wipe away for all time the stigma of inferiority for his Pacifics that had persisted in some quarters since the unhappy events of 1925. So far as the Anglo-Scottish accelerations were concerned, the East Coast Route was largely bound by the 'gentleman's agreement' with the West Coast on minimum time between London and Edinburgh concluded after the 'ninety-five'. There was also a tacit understanding following the brief competition with the Midland in 1910 that Leeds should not be the object of any appreciable competitive time-cutting by the routes from Kings Cross and St Pancras.

It was in the spirit of the national determination to climb out of the economic débâcle of 1931 that the first major breakaway from the Anglo-Scottish understanding of thirty-seven years earlier took place. It set the LMS and the LNER on a programme of acceleration that was to have the most dramatic results. There was indeed no knowing to what extent high-speed running might have progressed had not war once more come upon us in the autumn of 1939. The summer services of 1932 were no more than a mild curtain-raiser as to what was to follow. They saw both the LMS and the LNER beginning to climb away from the time-honoured 61·5mph fastest start-to-stop run. The LMS had the run of the 5.25pm up Liverpool flyer, booked from Crewe to Willesden, 152·7 miles in 142 minutes, 64·4mph, while the popular breakfast-car express from Leeds to Kings Cross was allowed no more than 100 minutes for the 105·5 miles up from Grantham, 63·4mph. In passing it is interesting to see that the trains chosen for preferential treatment by the northern companies were first-class businessmen's trains, in contrast to the mid-afternoon flight of the Cheltenham Flyer.

Preparations for acceleration on a much more ambitious scale began in November 1934. Even at that early stage in railway history the possibilities of very high-speed service by diesel traction was being demonstrated in both Germany and the USA, and it was attracting good business. Gresley had travelled by the Flying Hamburger and been very impressed with the speed and smoothness of riding. Far from being a diehard protagonist of steam traction, as he had sometimes been represented, he was sufficiently enthusiastic to invite the manufacturers of the German train to submit possible schedules for similar trains between London and Leeds, and London and Newcastle. The major criticism of the diesel rail-car units was that the passenger accommodation was considerably more cramped than that to which travellers from Kings Cross were accustomed, and when account was taken of the various permanent speed restrictions the average speeds that the German manufacturers could promise were much less than those currently being operated between Berlin and Hamburg. Gresley was very disappointed at the result of this investigation, and it was at this stage that

Sir Ralph Wedgwood, Chief General Manager of the LNER, suggested that better could be done with an ordinary steam Pacific hauling standard stock.

Arrangements were duly made for the running of a high-speed test from Kings Cross to Leeds with a train having approximately the same passenger accommodation as the Flying Hamburger, but with the latest type of LNER main line stock. This involved the running of no more than three coaches: a 'corridor first', a combined first-diner and kitchen car, and a brake-composite. To these were added the dynamometer car to provide complete technical coverage of the locomotive performance. With the few persons on board the gross load behind the tender did not exceed 147 tons. For this test run a path was prepared to provide for non-stop runs between Kings Cross and Leeds in 2¾ hours, in each direction – an average speed of 67·5mph. Having regard to the difficulties of the route north of Doncaster this was an ambitious schedule, even with so light a load and a Pacific engine to haul it. The choice of locomotive was at first sight surprising – a low-pressure A1, instead of one of the later high-pressure Super Pacifics of Class A3; but emphasis was laid upon the desirability of making the trip with standard equipment. At that time the A1 and A3 engines were used turn and turn about in the top-link duties, although the Kings Cross units then had their regular drivers. Rostered to do the same work the A3s were nevertheless generally considered to be superior in performance to the A1s. As the test of 30 November 1934 was staged as a demonstration of the practicability of a high-speed schedule rather than to break records it was therefore logical to use a locomotive of the inferior variety in the links that would be involved if the haulage of such a train became a daily task. Furthermore, despite the historic glamour attached to the name, engine No 4472 *Flying Scotsman* was not then considered to be the best of the A1s stationed at Kings Cross. On the other hand her regular driver, W. Sparshatt, was one of the hardest-running men in the link, and although a schedule of 165 minutes had been laid down for the 185·8 mile run he was instructed to get to Leeds as quickly as he could, paying strict regard, of course, to all speed regulations.

The result was a gain of thirteen minutes on the schedule laid down; the actual time from start to stop was 151min 56sec representing an average speed from start to stop of 73·4mph. This was an absolute record for the run from Kings Cross to Leeds, but the maximum speed reached down the 1 in 200 descent from Stevenage to Three Counties did not exceed 94¾mph. With such a light load it was natural that some fast work was done uphill, and Stoke Summit was cleared at a minimum speed of 81mph, but including the tender with the train the locomotive was hauling only 2·2 times its own weight, compared with approximately 3 times on the record run of the Cheltenham Flyer, and the most celebrated runs of the 'ninety-five'. That the thoughts of the management of the LNER were upon the commercial prospects of high speed rather than of record breaking for its own sake was shown by the immediate sequel. Having gained thirteen minutes on the 2¾-hour schedule going down it was decided to add two more coaches to the train for the up journey, making a trailing load of 207½ tons gross, or on this previous basis of comparison 2·86 times the weight of the locomotive. In this direction, of course, a major point of interest was to be the descent of the Stoke bank. No more favourable racing existed anywhere in the country, and everyone on the LNER, from Gresley himself downwards, had eyes on the legendary 102mph of *City of Truro* dating from 1904, which was then generally, if somewhat reluctantly, accepted as the world's record speed with steam traction. I have explained earlier how the 102 must be considered as questionable, though 100 can now be accepted.

On the London–Leeds trials of 1934 there was a massive double check on all that transpired. The dynamometer car produced a continuous record of the speed, as well as other details of the engine performance, while Cecil J. Allen was travelling as official recorder. It was not to be expected that so fast an overall time would be made on the up journey, with the heavier load; nevertheless the time of 157min 17sec start to stop represented a magnificent piece of running. In view of the maximum speed of 94¾mph going down it was evident that the engine would need not a little persuasion if something faster was to be obtained, descending from Stoke towards Peterborough. Up the 1 in 200 which extends for just over five miles from Grantham to the summit box the speed was 68½mph. The engine was pressed hard down the ensuing descent. There was no question of allowing the natural maximum speed to develop; the point of steam cut-off in the cylinders was made progressively later, and before Essendine speed reached very nearly if not quite to the magic 100mph. There was disagreement between the two principal sources of recording. Cecil J. Allen clocked two alternate quarter miles at speeds of 97·3mph, whereas the dynamometer car chart showed a marked but rather unnatural peak of exactly 100. Allen himself, in a very full write-up of the day's work in *The Railway Magazine,* definitely played down the maximum speed, and quoted 98mph in his log. He highlighted the considerably finer achievement that in this one day an aggregate distance of 250 miles had been covered at an average speed of 80mph. This and the London–Leeds time on the down journey stand as undisputed new records, but so far as maximum speed is concerned there was as much uncertainty over *Flying Scotsman*'s record down the Stoke bank as there was over the *City of Truro*'s down Wellington bank thirty years earlier.

The doubt over which company had the honour of the maximum speed record did not remain for long. In March 1935 the LNER carried their preparations for high-speed service a stage further with a dynamometer test run from Kings Cross to Newcastle and back, non-stop in each direction in the level four hours. A load of six coaches was conveyed, amounting to 217 tons gross behind the tender, and on this occasion one of the Super-Pacifics was used, No

2750 *Papyrus.* On the down run she was worked by her regular driver, H. Gutteridge, and on the return by the fire-eating Sparshatt. The circumstances were made more difficult for both engine crews because of a derailment of a freight train at Arksey, which entailed a short spell of single-line working between Doncaster and Shaftholme Junction. The train had covered the 138·6 miles from Kings Cross to Retford in 115¼ minutes, and was then 3¾ minutes ahead of the special schedule; but the subsequent delays involved a loss of 7 minutes. By some fine running the loss was fully recovered and Newcastle was reached 3 minutes early. The exact overall time was 237min 7sec for 268·3 miles, a new record average for this run of 68mph. The maximum speed did not exceed 88½mph, and it was notable that so fine an average could have been made without any exceptionally high speed. Taking the delay into account the net average speed from London to Newcastle was 70·2mph.

After the arrival in Newcastle at 1.3pm the return trip was timed to start at 3.47pm with the same engine. It was not to be expected that the delays from the derailment of the freight train would have been eliminated by the same evening, and so some time was got in hand to offset any such trouble. Shaftholme Junction, 108·1 miles, was passed in 99 minutes, 4 minutes early. No stop was required in this direction, merely a dead slow run over track newly repaired, and the four minutes in hand were just enough to offset this slowing. It was generally anticipated that a determined attempt to create a new world's record for steam would be made down the Stoke bank, and it was therefore no surprise to the experienced recorders in the train that no more than moderate speed was run between Doncaster and Grantham, keeping exactly to the 42-minute schedule set down for this 50·5 miles. The engine was clearly being nursed for an exceptional effort between Grantham and Peterborough. The former station was passed at 71½mph and the speed up the 5·4 miles to Stoke box was almost exactly the same as that of *Flying Scotsman* on the return Leeds test run in the previous November. The speeds on passing Stoke summit were 68½mph by *Flying Scotsman* and 69½mph by *Papyrus*. Then, as everyone had hoped, the previous record was literally shattered.

The point-to-point average speeds tell the story more vividly than pages of description:

Distance miles		Time m s	Point to Point Average Speed mph
0·0	Stoke Box	0 00	—
3·0	Corby	2 12	81·8
7·9	Little Bytham	5 13	96·9
11·5	Essendine	7 16	105·4
15·3	Tallington	9 32	100·6
18·2	Helpston Box	11 27	90·8
20·6	Werrington Junction	13 10	83·9

This time there was no question of peak rates over single quarter miles. The speed averaged 100·6mph for over *twelve miles*, from Corby to Tallington, and this time there was no disagreement about the maximum; the dynamometer car record and Cecil J. Allen's stop-watches both showed the splendid figures of 108mph. As with *Flying Scotsman*'s effort in the previous November however it was not a natural maximum. To maintain 69–70mph up the 1 in 200 from Grantham to Stoke box the engine was working in 28 per cent cut-off with full regulator; on topping the summit this was reduced to 22 per cent, but this did not produce so rapid an acceleration as was desired, and when at Corby station the speed had reached no more than 90mph an increase to 27 per cent was made, and at 95mph a further to 30 per cent. This put the speed over the 100; but after a mile of running at 102mph the cut-off was further increased to 32 per cent, and this produced the maximum of 108mph at the foot of the 1 in 200 gradient below Little Bytham. This tremendously exciting spurt put the train 5¼ minutes early through Peterborough; but far from showing any distress or fatigue after this effort, it prefaced some exceptionally hard and sustained running over the last 76·4 miles to Kings Cross, and this distance took only 62min 5 sec. Thus despite the delay over the site of the Arksey derailment Kings Cross was reached in 231¾ minutes – yet another new record.

That 108 was stirring news for all railway enthusiasts, but publication later of details of the engine working necessary to attain it left a rather uncomfortable feeling in the minds of those familiar with the normal working of the Gresley locomotives with the conjugated valve gear and derived motion for the valves of the inside cylinder. This performance, and that of *Flying Scotsman* in the previous November, differed from all previous British maximum speed records in that they were deliberate, officially inspired attempts at a record maximum. It is true that many of the speeds already quoted in this book were the results of close collaboration between expert recorders like Rous-Marten and the drivers concerned, and that high authority was not uninterested in the outcome; but they were achieved on the side, and sometimes the results had to be suppressed for a little time. With the Gresley Pacifics 4472 and 2750 the locomotives had to be extended far beyond their natural method of working at such speeds. The normal maximum speed down the Stoke bank for both A1 and A3 engines was around 92 or 93mph. To get the higher speeds attained on the experimental runs much longer cut-offs than normal had to be used, and with the conjugated gear this led to considerable over-running of the valves of the inside cylinder, giving far longer cut-offs than the nominal value working in the outside cylinders, and resulting in the inside cylinders doing a disproportionately high share of the total work. This in turn imposed a very high load on the inside connecting rod and crankshaft. *Flying Scotsman* was working at a nominal *forty per cent* when she approached 100mph in November 1934. Heaven knows what the actual cut-off was on the inside cylinder!

This is not to play down the glory of the maximum speeds attained either by *Flying Scotsman* or *Papyrus*, but rather to emphasise that they were unnatural, special feats, not essential in the case of *Papyrus* to the making of the great long-distance record which was to her everlasting distinction. Her actual average speed over the 15·3 miles from Corby to Helpston box was 99·2mph. Had she been working normally, and averaged 90mph over this stretch, the time would have been one minute longer, and this could easily have been regained by harder and *normal* running between Retford and Grantham, where the engine was being nursed, while the fire was being prepared for the all-out effort down the Stoke bank. This aside, the memorable day ended with *Papyrus* having made four World Records, as follows:

1. 500 miles in one day (Kings Cross to Croxdale and Croxdale back to Kings Cross) covered in 423min 57sec, inclusive of all checks, giving an average speed of 70·7mph. If allowance is made for the unexpected and exceptional delay due to the freight train derailment, the net time comes down to 412½ minutes, an average of 72·7mph.
2. 300 actual miles of one round trip covered at an average speed of 80mph.
3. A continuous stretch of 12·3 miles run at an average speed of 100·6mph.
4. The maximum speed of 108mph.

Although this book is concerned only with British achievements it may be mentioned that in the year 1935 the highest speed record fully authenticated anywhere else in the world had been 103mph on the Milwaukee road in the USA; so that *Papyrus* not only had shot ahead of the previous British feats of *Flying Scotsman* and *City of Truro*, but had left all other competitors well behind, the world over.

The trial runs left the most pleasurable anticipations, because at the Annual General Meeting of the LNER company, held very shortly after the runs, the chairman gave the first indication that regular services at this level of average speed were likely to be introduced between Kings Cross and Newcastle in the autumn of that same year. Connoisseurs of the LNER locomotive performance had no doubts as to the practicability of such schedules. The net times of the experimental runs on 5 March had shown gains of 10 minutes going north, and more than 12 minutes on the return journey. With such a load and such locomotives there seemed ample margin to include an intermediate stop at Darlington within the overall time of four hours between Kings Cross and Newcastle. The introduction of a batch of nine further A3 Pacifics, incorporating certain detailed improvements in design, earlier in the year seemed to assure an adequate motive-power stud for the additional services contemplated.

Nevertheless the dynamometer car records obtained with locomotives of both A1 and A3 classes tested in continuous high-speed running, and the occasional attainment of very high maximum speeds, had provided the locomotive department with data of the utmost importance. On the strength of this Gresley decided that for the regular maintenance of such fast schedules certain basic changes in design were desirable. Thermodynamically these changes were higher boiler pressure, smaller cylinders, larger diameter piston valves. On this basis Doncaster Works were launched into the production of the A4 class.

This is not a treatise on locomotive design; but the bare records of achievement would be hollow without some reference to the contributory factors. And when it came to maximum speed running there proved to be so phenomenal a difference between the A3 and A4 Pacifics that even the basic changes enumerated in the preceding paragraph do not provide more than a fraction of the answer. The external streamlining of the A4s strongly advocated by Bulleid, extolled by the neophytes, and regarded with amused tolerance by Gresley himself contributed another fraction; but it was the *internal* streamlining, of steam passages, ports and valves in the style of André Chapelon, that combined with the basic changes in thermodynamic proportions to make the A4s, by an immense margin, the freest-running locomotives yet seen on British metals.

How the trial run of the new Silver Jubilee express came to be made on 27 September 1935 is no part of the present theme. Here I am concerned only with the records that were made, and that showed at once the outstanding success with which Gresley and his staff had produced a high-speed locomotive.

In bare outline the first of the new locomotives, No 2509 *Silver Link*, hauling a gross trailing load of 230 tons, passed slowly through Peterborough station, 76·4 miles from Kings Cross, in 55 minutes 2 seconds, having averaged 83·3mph from the dead start. By comparison *Flying Scotsman* with her four-coach train of 147 tons took 60min 39sec for the same stretch of line, and *Papyrus* running non-stop to Newcastle took 63min 21 sec. In making the startling new record time to Peterborough *Silver Link* twice attained a maximum speed of 112½mph. Data for data this would seem no more than a natural improvement upon the achievement of *Papyrus*, with her attainment of 108mph. Actually there was all the difference in the world. *Silver Link* attained, and sustained for a long distance, her very high speeds on a normal running cut-off, working continuously from Woolmer Green onwards at between 15 and 18 per cent. There was never the slightest attempt to press the engine to attain a specially high maximum. The changes in design between the A3 and A4 classes had advanced the normal maximum from 90mph range to 110-plus! There was no dynamometer car attached to the train on 27 September 1935; the running was logged in his usual meticulous detail by Cecil J. Allen. On that ever-memorable afternoon the following World Records were captured by *Silver Link*; of these the first two were for either steam or diesel traction:

1. 25 miles continuously at or over 100mph. This was between Mileposts 30 and 55 covered in 13min 57sec at an average of 107·5mph.
2. 41·2 miles, Hatfield to Huntingdon, covered at an average speed of 100·6mph.
3. For steam traction only: 70 miles, from Wood Green to Fletton Junction, covered at an average speed of 91·8mph.

Strange as it may seem at first the maximum speed of 112½mph could not be claimed as anything but a British record. In between the 108 of *Papyrus* and the 112½ of *Silver Link*, a new German fully streamlined 4–6–4 locomotive, on test between Berlin and Hamburg, had been recorded at 119½mph. While this did not, apparently, form part of a long-sustained high-speed run it was accepted as fully authenticated. Nevertheless the 112½ of *Silver Link* was significant beyond all measure; for it represented the normally attained parameter of maximum speed of the new locomotives, in the same way as the Castle class locomotives on the GWR Cheltenham Flyer, at around 90mph, represented normally attained maxima. The astonishing freedom in running of the A4 locomotives was a matter of some concern, indeed, to the operating authorities, and drivers of the Silver Jubilee express were under the strictest instructions not to exceed 90mph. The four engines of the class were fitted with recording speedometers, and the charts giving a continuous record were most carefully scrutinised at headquarters.

The next step in the advancement of the British railways speed record once again concerned a Gresley Pacific, but it was as unpremeditated as those of *Flying Scotsman* and *Papyrus* were carefully planned. And it nearly ended in disaster! In the summer of 1936 first considerations were on hand for a high-speed streamlined service between Kings Cross and Edinburgh, and on 27 August dynamometer car test runs were arranged on the Silver Jubilee express to measure the engine performance in the most comprehensive detail, and ascertain the margin in reserve. The proposed Anglo-Scottish streamliner was to be a considerably heavier train than the Silver Jubilee. The addition of the dynamometer car to the standard train formation brought the gross trailing load up to 270 tons. On the southbound run the engine was No 2512 *Silver Fox*, manned by Driver G. H. Haygreen and Fireman C. Fisher. Haygreen was a most immaculate timekeeper, and before the start he was not advised that anything exceptional was expected. Nor was it, until Edward Thompson went through the corridor tender, somewhere around Grantham, and stood behind Haygreen on the left-hand side of the footplate. They topped Stoke summit at around 70mph, as *Flying Scotsman* and *Papyrus* had done, and were proceeding normally down towards Peterborough when Thompson suddenly said: 'Top a hundred.' By that time the train was passing Corby, at about 85mph – considerably slower than *Papyrus* at that station – and the boiler was quite unprepared for an exceptional effort.

Orders were orders, however, and Haygreen opened out. From the 96th milepost speed began leaping up. The 100 was reached near the 93rd milepost, and then, with cut-off gradually increased to no less than 35 per cent, the speed also went on increasing until a maximum was attained as far south as the 86th milepost – almost to Tallington Station. Cecil J. Allen clocked one half mile at 113·9mph, but the dynamometer car chart gave no more than 113mph and this was accepted as the new LNER and British record. But it was obtained at no small price. The tremendous punishment meted out to the machinery of the locomotive, in working at such long cut-offs at high speed, took its toll. The centre big-end not only heated, but at Hatfield completely disintegrated; a cylinder end was knocked out, and the crew were adjectively lucky to be able to continue gently on two cylinders only and to bring the train into Kings Cross – late maybe, but without having to stop. I knew Haygreen and his family well, and years afterwards, when he retired, he said:

'If only they had told me earlier what they wanted . . .!' The critical point was that unlike the runs of *Flying Scotsman* and *Papyrus*, Haygreen had a trainload of fare-paying passengers behind him. This maximum of 113mph remains today the highest ever attained by a British steam locomotive in revenue-earning service.

Flying Scotsman, *Papyrus*, *Silver Link* and *Silver Fox* were indeed the 'shooting stars', the meteorites of the Gresley firmament, even if the experience with *Silver Fox* had shown a weakness in the three-cylinder engine layout. But A1s, A3s and A4s alike were free-running express passenger thoroughbreds, and the records they made for the British steam locomotive, each in their several turns, stand for all time: the London–Leeds record stood to *Flying Scotsman*, the London–Newcastle to *Papyrus*, while to *Silver Link* there stood that amazing run from Kings Cross to Peterborough.

CHAPTER TEN

EAST-WEST CONTEST

UNTIL THE late autumn of 1936 the LNER had the field to itself in the making of new high-speed records. It is of course true that so far as start-to-stop average speeds were concerned the Great Western record of 1932 with the Cheltenham Flyer had not been seriously challenged with its speed of 81·6mph from Swindon to Paddington; but had the Silver Jubilee of September 1935 stopped at Peterborough instead of going on to Grantham, a start-to-stop average of around 83mph would have been easily possible. It was, of course, not the Great Western that constituted the most likely rival to the LNER in the brilliant programme upon which the latter company had become engaged; and up to this point the LMS had stood completely aside. In fact certain responsible officers had made it clear that they desired no part in a competition with lightly loaded ultra-high-speed trains. The principal business expresses of the LMS, timed for the most part at end-to-end speeds of 55 to 60mph, were loaded heavily and profitably, and the chief concern of the locomotive department had been to provide enhanced engine power to operate these heavy trains without recourse to double heading.

One can appreciate that such a policy was amply justified so long as services on which the LMS had a monopoly were unaffected by the LNER accelerations. It is true that the very first experimental run made by the LNER had been to Leeds; but this had not been followed up by a regular service, and in any case the Midland line from St Pancras was important to the LMS more for its intermediate business than for a through London–Leeds clientele. In Newcastle, served so brilliantly by the Silver Jubilee, the LMS were not interested, so far as London traffic was concerned. In the summer of 1936 however the LNER had begun active investigations towards the extension of the high-speed streamlined services into Scotland. With a well established run of four hours between Kings Cross and Newcastle it seemed a relatively simple matter to cover the remaining 124·4 miles to Edinburgh in a little under two hours, and provide a six-hour service between the two capital cities. The dynamometer car test runs on the Silver Jubilee itself, made on 27 September 1936, were followed on the next Saturday by a special trip from Newcastle to Edinburgh and back. The streamlined train not running on Saturdays was available in Newcastle and to this, as on 27 September, was added the dynamometer car. The 124·4 miles were covered in 118 minutes going north, and in 114 minutes on the return. The latter time closely approached the record run of the North Eastern 4-4-0 No 1620, in the closing stages of the 'ninety-five'.

His Majesty King George V had died in January 1936 and the first railway announcement in connection with the coronation of the new monarch was made by the LMS in the autumn of 1936, when the intention was stated of naming a Pacific engine of the Princess Royal class *Coronation*, in continuance of the precedent set by the London & North Western Railway in 1911. The George the Fifth class 4-4-0 that had borne that famous name for twenty-five years was, in 1936, shortly to be withdrawn, and it was explained at some length that this withdrawal would take place before the new Pacific was christened; so that the old 4-4-0, then numbered 25348 and stationed at Chester, would not actually be deprived of her name. In passing it is of interest to recall that when the LMS announcement was made the coronation anticipated in the late spring of 1937 was that of King Edward VIII. His abdication had yet to come. Before the end of the year two further railway events of outstanding importance took place. First, the LNER announced that in 1937 two more high-speed streamlined services would be introduced. One of these was the expected six-hour service to Edinburgh by a train to be named the Coronation and the other was a train to cover the London–Leeds route in 2¾ hours, to the schedule laid down for the experimental runs made with *Flying Scotsman* in 1934. Secondly, the LNER announcements had scarcely been made before the LMS staged two of the most remarkable high-speed long-distance runs that had ever been made with a steam locomotive.

The new LNER services were a straightforward logical development of the Silver Jubilee standards of performance – or so we thought at the time! The LMS, on the other hand, provided us with a mass of highly interesting and record-breaking statistics of actual performance on the road. Long before the public announcement of the impending LNER six-hour service the intention was known well enough in railway circles; in face of it the LMS could no longer stand aside, and reply only by hauling trains of gargantuan weight over Shap and Beattock with one locomotive. The natural reply would have been a six-hour service between London and Glasgow, and it was to test the practicability of this that a remarkable round trip of nearly 803 miles was made on 16 and 17 November 1936. For these runs, northbound one day and southbound the next, not only was a six-hour schedule laid down, but the 401·4-mile journey was in each direction to be made *non-stop*. This was not the first time the LMS had made a non-stop run between Euston and Glasgow. It had been done once previously, on a schedule more than two hours slower, by the 4-6-0 locomotive No 6113 *Cameronian* in April 1928. Why, other than for demonstration purposes, the trial runs of November 1936 should have been made non-stop is not clear. It imposed a severe task upon the engine crew, and one that was certainly not likely to be required in ordinary service. The LMS had no such things as corridor tenders, and those who manned the engine at Euston were there for 401·4 miles! But ours is not now to question why. Instead we can delight in the details of the magnificent performances put up on the two successive days.

It is no exaggeration to say that these two runs were planned in greater detail than any previous record runs in British railway history. R. A. Riddles, as Principal Assistant to the Chief Mechanical Engineer, had since 1935 taken personal charge of the development of the Stanier Pacifics so far as their utilisation in new and accelerated duties were concerned, and he alone was going to ride on the footplate with the engine crew on 16 and 17 November. With the driver and fireman there was to travel a passed-fireman, as reserve engineman fully qualified to drive or fire as necessary. It was however not enough for Riddles to have the schedule set out in complete detail, with passing times laid down for nearly forty intermediate points in each direction. The drawing office had prepared a chart showing the speeds that were necessary for time-keeping over every mile of the route, paying strict regard to all the prescribed speed restrictions and the accelerative capacity of the locomotive intermediately. The test train included the Horwich dynamometer and six of the latest main line corridor coaches, making a gross load of 230 tons behind the tender. This was almost exactly the weight of the Silver Jubilee train in revenue-earning service. A chart covering 400 miles of line would have been an impossibly unwieldy thing to have handled on the footplate in the ordinary way; so Riddles had made, to his design, a tray that he could carry pedlar-fashion, suspended by straps passing round the back of his neck, and at each side of this tray were cylinders capable of being revolved. The chart was mounted on one of these, and slowly wound from one to the other as the journey proceeded. Riddles thus had constantly before him a reminder of the speed at which they should be running to keep the six-hour schedule. On such a long and arduous run such an aid to timekeeping was invaluable. It is perhaps characteristic of the modesty of the distinguished engineer concerned that in the highly eulogistic accounts of the run that appeared in the *Railway Magazine* at the time there was no mention, even, of Riddles's presence on the footplate at all, let alone of the ingenious vade-mecum that he had with him.

The engine chosen for this highly important occasion was No 6201 *Princess Elizabeth*, the second of the Stanier Pacifics, retaining the original boiler, but then fitted with a 32 element superheater. In addition to the continuous record obtained with the instruments in the dynamometer car the running was logged in complete detail by Mr D. S. M. Barrie, now retired from the high office of Chairman and General Manager of the Eastern Region of British Railways. On the outward journey the test train began to draw ahead of the schedule laid down after Rugby. Crewe, 158·1 miles, was passed in 132min 52sec, and *Hardwicke*'s famous record of 126min for the 141 miles from Crewe to Carlisle in the 'ninety-five' was lowered to 122min 32sec. Both stations were passed slowly through at 20mph. To Carlisle the speed from the start had averaged 70·2mph. The maximum had been 95½mph descending from Tring towards Bletchley; but in addition to the major restrictions at Rugby, Stafford, Crewe and Preston, speed had to be considerably reduced at no fewer than twenty-eight places between Euston and Carlisle. Speed limits which were of no consequence in ordinary working had a decidedly hampering effect at the speed the special train was being run. Of these may be mentioned particularly 62mph at Hincaster junction and 60mph at Oxenholme, which between them completely precluded an all-out attack on Grayrigg bank. Fortunately it was not so with Shap. Tebay was passed at 78½mph and the summit cleared at 57mph. The train was 4½minutes early on the test schedule on passing through Carlisle, and except for a slack to 58mph over Gretna Junction the running was completely unhindered until well over Beattock Summit.

Seeing that engine and crew had been hard at work for 4½ hours when Carlisle was passed the performance over the

Caledonian line was quite outstanding. While old records had been handsomely beaten between Euston and Crewe, and narrowly beaten onwards to Carlisle, they were simply shattered over the 49·7 miles leading to Beattock summit. In the races of 1888 and 1895 the fastest times made were around 53 minutes – mighty good times too for the little Drummond 4-2-2 and 4-4-0 engines involved; but on 16 November 1936 *Princess Elizabeth* wiped off that distance in no more than 41min 42sec. On passing Beattock summit she had covered 348·8 miles from the Euston start in 297min 6sec, and was running practically nine minutes ahead of the special schedule. From the start the magnificent average of 70·5mph had been made, and up the last four miles of the Beattock bank speed had fallen only from 57½ to 56mph. Furthermore, although the load of 230 tons was light compared with the normal West Coast express standards the engine was nevertheless hauling 2·74 times its own weight. After a fast descent of the Upper Clyde valley, with a maximum speed of 83½mph, the final approaches to Glasgow were beset by many checks. Nevertheless the schedule allowed for such hindrances, and the train reached Glasgow Central just over six minutes inside the even six hours – 353min 38sec to be exact. This gave the record average speed over such a distance of 68·2mph. Mr E. J. H. Lemon, a Vice-President of the LMS, had travelled with the train, and he was so delighted with the performance that he suggested that they might try to make still faster time on the return journey. Riddles however countered this proposal with the suggestion that the locomotive capacity on hand could be better shown by taking a heavier load. This was agreed, and on the following morning they started out for Euston with 260 tons behind the tender.

Despite the extra load, despite a stormy winter's day, and despite a repair to the engine which had to be made at St Rollox, and which was of sufficient concern to keep Riddles up for most of the night, they cut nearly 9½ minutes off the previous day's times, and by reaching Euston in the astonishing time of 344¼min made a start-to-stop average speed over the whole distance of exactly 70mph. Carlisle, 102·3 miles, was passed in 93min 20sec, and then over the two sections of the LNW main line the times were 119min 57sec from Carlisle to Crewe, and 130min 58sec onwards to Euston. The respective average speeds on the three stages were 65·9, 70·5, and 72·4mph, and the flying average over the 364·5 miles from Carstairs to Wembley, covered in 298min 8sec, was 73·3mph. These average speeds were all the more remarkable in view of the number of speed restrictions that had to be observed. The maximum was 95mph – not as might be expected in descending from Beattock or Shap, but on the dead level approaching Crewe after the long gradual rise from Weaver Junction. The combined average speed resulting from the two days' running, of 802·8 miles in 698min 53sec, namely 69mph, set up a new long-distance world record for steam. As in the case of *Papyrus* on the LNER, in March 1935, it was made by a standard locomotive with standard rolling stock, and over a track certainly not prepared for continuous very fast running. The very detailed logs of the journeys published at the time show the running to be very much a succession of fits and starts, as brakes were applied to observe one speed restriction after another, and the engine vigorously accelerated afterwards. In the circumstances the management of the locomotive provided a most exacting job for both driver and fireman, and equally of course for the reserve engineer travelling with them and assisting when necessary. These men were all from Crewe North shed, where the top-link crews worked southwards to Euston and northwards to Glasgow and Perth in the course of their ordinary duties. The driver was T. J. Clarke, the fireman C. Fleet, and the reserve man Passed-Fireman Shaw.

With such performance on the record it was assumed, almost without question, that a six-hour service between London and Glasgow would be introduced in the summer of 1937. As on the LNER the experience of the high-speed runs with a standard Pacific engine indicated that for continuous work in ordinary service, with locomotives handled by every crew in a link rather than by picked men of outstanding calibre such as Clarke and Fleet, some changes in design were desirable. Stanier himself was in India at the time, and the responsibility for initiating the Coronation class of super-Pacific fell mainly upon Riddles and T. F. Coleman, who was then Chief Locomotive Draughtsman at CME headquarters, Derby. On the LMS the development from the Princess Royal class to the Coronations was more far-reaching than the transition from Class A3 to A4 on the LNER. In the latter case the chassis and the layout remained the same. With the LMS Pacifics the new variety had only two sets of valve gear, with the valves of the inside cylinders actuated by rocking shafts from the outside valve gear. The principles of internal streamlining were well and truly applied, and a locomotive of exceptional high-speed potential began to take shape on the drawing boards at Derby. In due course, however, to the intense disappointment of all West Coast supporters, it was announced that the new service to Glasgow would occupy 6½ hours, and not the even six hours as confidently anticipated. Allowing for the greater distance the overall average speed would be 61·7mph from London, as compared with 65·4mph of the forthcoming LNER streamliner from Kings Cross to Edinburgh.

Viewing the situation in retrospect there is no doubt that the LMS had taken the right and most prudent course. The trial runs of November 1936 had highlighted the number of locations at which reductions of speed would be required in an ultra-high speed service. The constant braking could be an annoyance to travellers accustomed to the traditional smoothness and comfort of the West Coast main line, while the manning of a very high-speed service could have presented its problems. The great majority of the enginemen would have been new to it, and, very wisely in my opinion, the management decided to work up to it gradually. Although this has nothing to do with the making of records there was another important difference between the policies of the LMS and the LNER in regard to the Anglo-Scottish streamliners of 1937, in that while the six-hour Coronation was to provide an entirely new facility in the form of a late-afternoon flyer from both London and Edinburgh, the Coronation Scot, as the LMS train was named, was a replacement of the Glasgow section of the time-honoured Mid-day Scot – the old Corridor of LNWR days. It is true that this latter train, with through portions from Edinburgh and Aberdeen – and as if this were not enough attaching a Plymouth–Glasgow section at Crewe – had been swelling to Brobdingnagian proportions, approaching the haulage limit of the Princess Royal class engines. The introduction of the Coronation Scot certainly provided some relief, in the regular running of a second train daily from London at that time of day.

While the daily schedule of the new train was not to be very exciting the approaching completion of the new locomotive at Crewe was accompanied by a tremendous wave of publicity. There is no doubt that the high management of the LMS felt that the LNER had enjoyed far too much of the limelight in recent years! The completion of the Coronation class Pacific provided a good opportunity for a hearty counterblast. We can forget the animated discussions that took place at the time about the relative merits of the streamlining of the rival Pacifics. There is no doubt that the *Coronation* engine, when she emerged from Crewe Works, created the appropriate sensation for the popular press, and this emergence was to be followed by a demonstration run for the press, technical and popular alike. However leisurely the ordinary schedule of the Coronation Scot train was to be there was certainly no intention to mince matters on the Invitation Run to Crewe and back, fixed for 29 June 1937. The fact that the LNER were throwing a similar party with the Coronation streamliner on the very next day added a good deal of spice to the LMS occasion. Those of us who were privileged to participate on 29 June were quite certain that if any new records were made between Euston and Crewe an all-out attempt to surpass them would be made on the following day. It was the atmosphere of the 'ninety-five' all over again.

So the special W700 set out from Euston, booked to run the 158·1 miles to Crewe in 135min at an average speed of 70·2mph. The driver of the new engine was again T. J. Clarke, and this time his fireman was C. Lewis. With them on the footplate was Inspector S. Miller of Willesden, and again Riddles himself. The speed restrictions were generally the same as those in force at the time of the trials in November 1936; but it was a fairly open secret that the LMS were out to capture the British railway speed record. The section of line between Norton Bridge and Crewe was specially fettled up, and the line maximum of 90mph lifted, to permit of a record attempt down the Madeley bank. The terrain and alignment were ideal – except in a respect that arose in dramatic and terrifying suddenness –and those on the footplate were asked to attempt something special. The British record then stood at 113mph, and I have since learned that the crew were asked to try to get 120. Without anything unusual in the way of running, and a very even pace uphill and down, the train passed Stafford just over five minutes early on the special schedule: 133·6 miles from Euston in 109min 56sec – 73mph. Then the engine was taken very quietly onwards until the 60 mph restriction through Norton Bridge was behind us; and then the attempt on the record began. Unfortunately it was ill judged. What I write now is, regrettably, being wise many years after the event; but had a speed chart been prepared for this critical section with the same care and scientific basis as that for the Euston–Glasgow runs of November 1936 the result might have been very different.

Seeing what had been done on the latter occasion in accelerating the *Princess Elizabeth* engine away after speed restriction, the recovery from the Norton Bridge slack on 29

June was disappointingly slow. I was travelling in the leading coach of the train, and one just could not hear the exhaust beat of the engine. As we topped Whitmore summit the speed was no more than 85mph. I appreciate that 'no more than 85mph' is in relative terms only; but knowing the capacity of these engines it could easily have been 95, and that would have made all the difference afterwards. Certainly the subsequent acceleration was very swift; but we were getting perilously near to Crewe before we approached the LNER record of 113mph. The entry to Crewe station, over three successive crossover roads, was reminiscent of the celebrated run through Portobello, Edinburgh, in the early hours of 20 August 1895, immortalised by the racy pen of Norman Doran Macdonald; and when we arrived safe and sound, in No 3 of all Crewe platforms, the stop-watch readings of four independent recorders, Cecil J. Allen, D. S. M. Barrie, S. P. W. Corbett and myself, all agreed precisely that the maximum speed had not exceeded 112½mph. No record could be claimed in this respect; but in quickly checking over his figures, while still on the platform, Cecil J. Allen remarked that the time from Milepost 157 to the stop in the station – 1·1 miles in 1min 19sec – *was* a record, and of such a nature that he added, 'Nobody will believe us when we tell them!' The overall time from Euston to Crewe was 129¾ minutes, an average of 73·1mph.

The large party of guests was entertained to lunch at the Crewe Arms Hotel. E. J. H. Lemon presided, and very wittily and successfully he made light of the somewhat precipitate entry into Crewe, which as one correspondent afterwards wrote 'strewed the floor of the dining car with a mosaic of broken crockery'. In the course of his speech however he was handed a slip of paper; it was the result of a scrutiny of the speed-recorder chart taken off the locomotive. Up to that point he had quoted the 112½mph agreed among the four of us, but as he read the paper a broad smile spread over his face, and he said: 'I have not been bribed, but I can now tell you that the maximum speed was

114mph.' It is, I am afraid, no exaggeration to say that those of us who had been taking, among us, so detailed an account of the running regarded this claim with some scepticism. We would all have readily agreed that a peak of 113mph could have occurred, although it had eluded *four* independent stop watches; but 114 took some stomaching, particularly as by this the British railway speed record was snatched by one mile per hour from the LNER. We had however little time to reflect on the ethics of the situation. The LMS had now officially claimed 114mph and we all made for the return special to Euston.

This time Riddles and his men went out for a different kind of record. Although the schedule time was again 135 minutes the engine was driven at a uniformly high speed, uphill and down, and without forcing the effort beyond a normal rate of steaming at any point they succeeded in anticipating the present electric standards of speed by reaching Euston in 119 minutes from Crewe. This gave an average speed from start to stop of 79·7mph – still not quite up to the Great Western 81·6mph of June 1932, but intrinsically an equal, if not finer, performance. The load in relation to engine weight was almost exactly the same, 2·95 (GWR) to 2·96 (LMS), and the ratios of load to tractive effort of the locomotives were 16·7 (GWR) and 17·9 (LMS). But whereas the Great Western had a completely clear run, the Coronation Scot had to observe the speed restrictions at Stafford and Rugby, and the reductions actually made were to 30mph in the first case and 40mph in the second. If, to assess the effects of these slacks, one deducts the distances and times taken between Great Bridgeford and Milford and then between Newbold Signal Box and Kilsby Tunnel North there is left 144·5 miles covered in 105min 51sec, or an average of 82mph. The actual flying average over the 152·6 miles from Milepost 155 to South Hampstead, including all slacks, was 82·8mph. Finest of all the various averages that can be worked out in respect of this splendid run was over the 69·9 miles from Welton to Willesden Junction covered in 47min

1sec, at an average of 89·3mph. The maximum speed was exactly 100mph at Castlethorpe troughs. On this memorable day, if the LMS did not secure to everybody's satisfaction the British railway speed record, they certainly claimed the fastest start-to-stop run yet made over a distance of 100 miles, and also that over 150 miles.

On the very next afternoon the LNER staged an Invitation Run with the Coronation train. This proved to be a much heavier proposition than the Silver Jubilee, and its nine coaches weighed 312 tons tare. As with the Silver Jubilee, Grantham was the nominal destination of the special run, and there can be little doubt that the firm intention of all LNER personnel concerned was to push their own speed record several points higher than the previous 113mph and regain without any doubt the Blue Riband claimed by so slender a margin by the LMS. On the down journey from Kings Cross, worked by one of the new Garter-blue A4s, the *Dominion of Canada,* the heavier streamlined train was run competently to the schedule, passing Grantham station, 105·5 miles, in 87½ minutes. The train then proceeded northwards to the Barkston triangle where it could be turned without detaching the locomotive or the picturesque beaver-tailed observation car at the rear end. A wait then had to be made at Barkston South until the time of the return trip to start. It was important not to get away before time, even though all was ready, to ensure getting a clear road throughout. That wait at Barkston was prejudicial in another way. The period of 'standing by' was a considerable break in the continuity of steaming of the boiler, and if a new record was to be made down the Stoke bank it was essential to pass the summit at or over 70mph. This meant a continuous uphill acceleration in hard steaming conditions immediately after the start from Barkston. It was the worst possible demand that could be made, not so much on the boiler as on the firebed. The engine was duly pounded up to Stoke, breasting the summit at 69mph, and then there was a race, in opposite directions – upwards by the speedometer needle, and downwards by the pressure gauge. The driver did his utmost, but with falling boiler pressure he could not get more than 109½mph, and so matters rested for another year.

Until the later summer of 1937 there had been three instances of exceptionally high speed by the A4 class LNER locomotives: the twice attained 112½mph of *Silver Link* on the inaugural trip; the 113mph of *Silver Fox* on the southbound dynamometer car trial in September 1936, and then the 109½mph of *Dominion of Canada* on the trial run of the Coronation. While *Silver Link*'s maxima had been attained in her stride, in normal but nevertheless ideal conditions of steaming, both the other instances resulted from attempts to force a high maximum in definitely unfavourable circumstances. From the viewpoint of making records this was doubly unfortunate, because the descent from Stoke summit towards Peterborough is in normal running one of the most favourable locations for record-making to be found anywhere on the British railway system. How favourable was most vividly shown on a journey I enjoyed as a passenger on the Coronation in August 1937. On that occasion the train was being worked by engine No 4491 *Commonwealth of Australia* with the usual nine coach load, 325 tons gross, behind the tender, and when Grantham was neared there was no question of working up for an exceptional effort. The steaming was quite steady, at an almost constant rate of evaporation, and after passing Grantham at 69mph speed fell away to 64½mph at Stoke summit. The driver then continued with the same method of working down to Peterborough. There was not the slightest attempt to secure a high speed. It was the inaugural run of *Silver Link* over again, but with a heavier load. We swept in effortless style up to 106mph and we continued running at between 104 and 106mph to the point of slowing a little for the water troughs at Werrington.

One is immediately prompted to ask what kind of speed might have been attained in these ideal circumstances if the engine *had* been opened out – not to the murderous extent of *Silver Fox* and *Dominion of Canada,* but perhaps from the actual 15 per cent which produced our 106mph to 18 or even 20 per cent. Of the record makers down the Stoke bank only the A3 engine *Papyrus* had the dual advantage of being fully nursed and ready for the attempt, and of doing it in the midst of a long spell of continuous steaming. The significance of my own service run on the Coronation can perhaps be better appreciated by the following figures:

Engine	*Gross Trailing Load tons*	*Max Speed mph*	*Av Speed mph Bytham–Werrington**
Papyrus	217	108	96·0
Silver Fox	270	113	98·4
Dominion of Canada	320	109½	92·4
Commonwealth of Australia	325	106	103·5

* 12·7 miles

Although passing Stoke summit some 5mph slower than the other three engines, *Commonwealth of Australia* made the fastest time of all over the 20·6 miles from Stoke box to Werrington Junction.

The summer of 1937 left us all with many reflections. It was generally considered that in the exciting contest that had been waged the honours were even between the LMS and the LNER. One reflection had been disturbing, namely that, as in more than one previous phase in British railway history, the capacity of locomotives for high speed had stepped ahead of the capacity for stopping! I need not go further into the technicalities of this situation than perhaps to add that on one occasion when I was travelling on the Coronation the driver of the A4 had to reverse the engine to avoid over-running an adverse signal, and that during many weekends in 1938 trials were being carried out on the Coronation train-set with an improved form of vacuum brake. These tests were indirectly connected with the next and final great event in the East–West speed contest of this period. No one who knew Sir Nigel Gresley personally expected for one moment that he would be prepared to accept indefinitely the situation remaining from the events of 29 and 30 June 1937. In the meantime also the German State Railways had set up a new world record for steam with a speed of 125mph by a newly fully streamlined 4-6-4 locomotive. There was therefore a dual challenge which Gresley covertly accepted, namely to regain the British record, so narrowly snatched from him by LMS, and if at all possible to regain for Britain the world record.

There was good reason for maintaining a great deal of secrecy about the preparations. The mere idea of a train running at 125mph or more would have turned some contemporary officers of the LNER aghast. Most fortuitously that continuing series of brake trials provided a cloak. By the late spring of 1938 the running of the Coronation train-set from Kings Cross on Sundays was becoming quite a frequent occurrence. The operating department was asked to provide the necessary paths so that the test train could be stopped from various speeds in different conditions of gradients. Sometimes the distance available to work up speed to the required value was relatively short, and to provide the accelerative power and also the ability to run at 90mph the engine of the test train was always an A4. Locomotive Inspector Jenkins of Kings Cross was nearly always in charge on the footplate. A test was arranged for 3 July 1938. The preliminaries were quite normal and the brake testing team of the Westinghouse Brake and Signal Company was briefed as usual. Features that were unusual, to be noted by any experienced onlooker at Kings Cross, were the inclusion of the dynamometer car in the train, and the use of a Doncaster engine, No 4468 *Mallard*, instead of the usual Kings Cross engine. It was not until the train was actually under way that my Westinghouse colleagues learned of the real purpose of the trip. Gresley was out for nothing less than a world record. As on all previous special LNER runs Cecil J. Allen had been invited to travel; but on this occasion he was unable to attend. The recording was thus solely by the dynamometer car, though this of course provided a record of unquestionable accuracy.

The train went through to Grantham, and as with the Coronation trial of 30 June 1937 was turned on the Barkston triangle. Then when the appointed time came they 'went in a perisher' for it – to quote a memorable phrase of Charles Rous-Marten. There was no question of allowing the engine to make her own pace on normal cut-offs; she was pressed to the limit – as it turned out, in fact, a little beyond it! The driver gradually advanced the cut-off till *Mallard* was working on 40 per cent – *forty per cent* – at over 120mph! By this merciless pounding they succeeded in getting the world record, with a speed of 126mph near Essendine. But the mighty effort took its toll, and the Achilles' heel of the Gresley three-cylinder engines, the middle big-end, failed. The engine was eased down considerably; the train was stopped at New England, where it was found necessary to take *Mallard* off the train. While like many famous British victories it was a close-run thing it secured for the LNER and for Great Britain the world record with steam traction. Today we can be assured that this record will stand for all time.

CHAPTER ELEVEN

LESSER RECORDS OF THE 'THIRTIES'

WHILE THE Pacific locomotives of the northern lines were adding such lustre to the pages of British locomotive history in the later nineteen thirties some notable achievements in other directions must not pass unnoticed. None of these were records in the sense that they surpassed previous values of maximum speed or of start-to-stop averages; but they were records for the type of locomotives concerned, or in some cases for the particular stretch of line. Since the very early years of the century when the Brighton was making its fast experimental runs with the Billinton B4 class, and the South Western were pushing things to the point of a fatal recklessness in the working of the American specials from Plymouth, the Southern had largely dropped out of the picture.

There had been one or two isolated instances of maximum speeds of 90mph or just over, with both the Urie and the King Arthur classes of 4-6-0 and with the Lord Nelsons, but nothing to excite special attention. Observers could not fail to notice however that the original Urie version of the N15 class, modified only in respect of the draughting, was consistently as fast as if not faster than the King Arthur class proper on the downhill stretches of the Salisbury–Exeter main line.

From the earliest Drummond days the fine stretch of line east of Battledown Junction had been a favourite racing ground for up LSWR expresses, and at one time the company had a start-to-stop run from Basingstoke to Vauxhall that could have developed into a Cheltenham Flyer schedule, so favourable were the gradients, and so free the line from restrictions except for the final approach through Clapham Junction. But this schedule, 46½ miles in 49 minutes at an average speed of 57mph, was not revived after the war, and it was to the eastbound run of the Atlantic Coast Express, non-stop from Salisbury to Waterloo, that one normally looked for the fastest sustained running on the Western Section of the Southern Railway. A record of the first magnitude stands to the credit of engine No 777 *Sir Lamiel*, of the King Arthur class. It is a record of such outstanding quality indeed that at least one very experienced locomotive engineer of the Southern who, in the course of his duties, had accumulated a vast footplate knowledge of the King Arthurs, found difficulty in believing it. His assessment was that it could have been achieved only with a strong following cross-wind! Atmospherics apart, the load of the train, the times achieved, and the speeds attained are authentic beyond any dispute. Weather conditions are all part of the luck of the game where the making of speed records is concerned. The direction of the wind has prevented records being made on many occasions, and if indeed it did contribute to the astonishing run of *Sir Lamiel* then good luck to the Southern.

The plain fact is that the Atlantic Coast Express, with ten coaches weighing 345 tons gross behind the tender, was taken over the 83·8 miles from Salisbury to Waterloo in 72min 41sec. The start-to-stop average speed was thus 69·2mph, which as far as can be traced is an absolute record for this stretch of line, with any class of locomotive. The route is, of course, far removed from a continuously favourable racing track. It starts indeed with a heavy climb over the eastern ridges of the Salisbury Plain, with a long stretch of 1 in 140; and although the ensuing descent to Andover can be taken with no restraint it is followed by a long gradual ascent to the summit of line near Oakley. It is only then, when 31·4 miles out of Salisbury, that really favourable conditions begin, and continue without a break to the approaches to Clapham Junction. The journey can therefore be sub-divided into four sections:

1. The initial ascent from Salisbury to Grateley.
2. Grateley to Oakley, including the Andover dip and long subsequent rise.
3. The sustained fast stretch from Oakley to Earlsfield.
4. The suburban approach to London, with heavily reduced speed through Clapham and Vauxhall.

Analysed thus, the performances of *Sir Lamiel* is dissected as follows:

	Distance miles	*Time m s*	*Av Speed mph*
Salisbury–Grateley	11·0	14 00	47·2
Grateley–Oakley	20·4	15 54	76·8
Oakley–Earlsfield	46·8	34 52	80·4
Earlsfield–Waterloo	5·6	7 55	42·4

For 60·8 miles of this exciting journey, from Grateley to Surbiton, speed averaged 80·4mph. Maximum rates were 88½mph at both Andover Junction and Hook, with an absolute maximim of exactly 90mph at Byfleet.

When O. V. S. Bulleid succeeded Maunsell as Chief Mechanical Engineer of the Southern his great interest in locomotives, as such, led him to make many footplate journeys to form a personal assessment of the locomotive stock that had become his responsibility. He dismissed the King Arthurs as an obsolescent design, very unnecessarily heavy for the work they did; but on the other hand he was delighted with the Schools. The King Arthurs, with their ultra-simple two-cylinder layout and all the machinery outside and readily accessible, were of course the precise pattern on which Riddles and his staff built the entire British Railways standard designs – with one solitary and unsuccessful exception. In the nineteen thirties the King Arthurs constituted the *only* British express passenger design of the grouping era with this layout, and it was diametrically opposed to Bulleid's avowed principles. He included the Schools in his programme of modernisation, fitting some of these engines with multiple jet blastpipes of the Lemaitre type; but although the modified examples proved free running they were not appreciably better than the original version. It was nevertheless one of the multiple jet engines that made the fastest down run ever recorded between Waterloo and Salisbury. With a nine-coach train of 305 tons, engine No 931 *King Wimbledon*, after taking 15min 20sec to cover the first 12 miles out to Surbiton, then averaged exactly 75mph over the 60·8 miles on to Grateley. Signal delays however spoiled the conclusion of the run. Apart from this Salisbury should have been reached in about 74 minutes from Waterloo.

To connoisseurs of locomotive performance, as distinct from the novelty of record breaking, nothing gives greater pleasure than to observe the continuing prowess of older types of locomotive in modern conditions; and when such locomotives are breaking their own records, if not necessarily making new ones of national or international status, it is an added delight. Such during the nineteen thirties was the case of the Great Northern large-boilered Atlantics. Until the year 1937 these engines had a monopoly of the London–Leeds Pullman trains. Picked units were allocated to Kings Cross and Leeds Copley Hill sheds specially for these duties, and the standards of running and general punctuality were very high. I had many runs on these trains in the years 1932 to 1937, and the very first time I personally clocked a maximum speed of 90mph was from the footplate of engine No 4423, near Arlesey, on the down Queen of Scots express. This was one of the Copley Hill stud – a splendid engine in pristine condition; but a far more remarkable experience came to me in returning to London on the same day. A minor defect had developed on the Kings Cross engine allocated to the corresponding up express. No spare Atlantic was available in Leeds, and no other suitable engine was on hand; so a spare was obtained, at a moment's notice, from Doncaster. This proved to be No 4456, and the London driver and fireman set out on this severe duty not knowing what kind of an engine this spare might turn out to be.

I have several times previously described the magnificent performance that ensued, with the fastest net time from Leeds to Kings Cross ever set on record with one of the Pullman trains of the inter-war period. Here I am primarily concerned with the attainment of the highest speed ever recorded with one of the Great Northern Atlantic engines, and how I saw it done from the footplate. By the time we were nearing Grantham it was evident that No 4456 was a very willing, free-steaming, and free-running engine. So much has been written in earlier chapters of this book about the descent from Stoke tunnel to Peterborough that it was extremely interesting to see the technique used on the Atlantic by a driver who was in a hurry. The water troughs at Werrington Junction were under repair, and it was necessary to stop at Peterborough to take water. This was going to cause some loss of time, unless we could make it up elsewhere, and the Stoke bank was accordingly put to good effect. By the time we passed Grantham, having been hard at work for over an hour, the steaming of the boiler was rock-steady. The firebed was in perfect shape, and as we climbed the 1 in 200 up to Stoke box, from Grantham, the engine was working in 35 per cent cut-off with the regulator about one-half open. This produced a steadily maintained minimum speed of 55mph on the bank. The load was one of seven Pullman cars, representing a gross load of 290 tons behind the tender.

The train was thus passing Stoke summit at about 15mph slower than the Pacifics on the various runs described earlier when very high maxima were attempted. The speed was roughly 10mph slower than on my own journey as a passenger on the Coronation. On passing Stoke summit the driver of No 4456 left the controls completely untouched. The regulator was one-half open, and the cut-off in 35 per cent. In the ten miles between mileposts 100 and 90 speed increased by no less than 38mph to a maximum of 93mph. It is interesting to compare this increase, with the engine left to accelerate without additional encouragement, to the Pacific runs discussed in previous chapters thus:

Engine	*Load tons gross*	*Speeds mph Stoke*	*Speeds mph Maximum*	*Increase mph*
Flying Scotsman	207	68½	98	29½
Papyrus	217	69	108	39
Silver Fox	270	68½	113	44½
Dominion of Canada	320	69	109	40
Commonwealth of Australia	325	64½	106	41½
Mallard	240	74½	126	51½
4-4-2 No 4456	290	55	93	38

It was certainly a very remarkable performance on the part of engine No 4456, and as with *Commonwealth of Australia* it was no mere flash in the pan, to be eased off the moment the maximum was attained between Little Bytham and Essendine. The veteran Atlantic continued running at 90mph right on to Tallington, and made the splendid average of 88mph over the 15·2 miles from Corby to Helpston signal box. Allowing for various slight checks en route, and for the effect of the stop at Peterborough to take water, the overall analysis of this run works out as follows:

LEEDS–KINGS CROSS

185·8 miles

Overall time	189min 35sec	58·8mph
Running time	184min 50sec	60·5mph
Net time	177min	63·0mph

While this does not approach the record time of *Flying Scotsman* on the experimental run of 30 November 1934, when the actual overall time was 157¼mins, the net time of 177 minutes was certainly a 'record of records' among the many notable performances of the Atlantics, doubly praiseworthy for being made by a hastily acquired spare engine, and a load that in relation to the nominal tractive power was practically double that conveyed on the racing Pacific runs. The maximum speed of 93mph is certainly the record for the Great Northern Atlantic engines.

Until the early months of 1939 the record time between London and Newcastle still stood at the 231 minutes 48 seconds made by the A3 engine *Papyrus* on the experimental run of 5 March 1935. In regular service the Silver Jubilee made a passenger stop at Darlington, and although the up Coronation was booked non-stop from Newcastle to Kings Cross in 237min any spectacular gains on schedule time with this train were not to be expected. Although the A4 class locomotives were regularly employed the load of 312 tons tare was practically fifty per cent greater than that of the Silver Jubilee; but a more critical factor was that the locomotive worked through between Edinburgh and London. This very severe task was without much doubt the most exacting duty ever set to British steam locomotives and their crews in the years before World War II. The coal supply was often critical and some instances actually occurred of the locomotives running completely out of coal before London was reached, and having to stop for assistance at Hitchin. The up Coronation was therefore always a test of enginemanship, and drivers were not inclined to press their locomotives unduly. Consequently so far as published records go no A4 succeeded in lowering the A3 record of *Papyrus* of which the net time of 227½ minutes was equivalent to an average speed of 70·8mph.

The week ending 25 March 1939 was a bad one in the history of A4 working on the up Coronation. Twice in that one week the booked engine failed and had to be taken off the train at Newcastle. But a week that saw two unfortunate contretemps chalked up against the A4s brought fresh renown to the A3s. During the winter months, when the journey of the Coronation was made almost entirely in darkness, the task of the locomotives was made a little easier by not running the beaver-tail observation car. The gross load was reduced to about 290 tons compared to the summer load of 325 tons. It was nevertheless a considerably harder haulage proposition than the test train of 5 March 1935, when *Papyrus* had a gross load of only 217 tons. But to come in more detail to March 1939: on the first of these occasions the train arrived punctually at Newcastle, and a defect on the A4 was discovered only when the Scottish driver climbed down to make the usual short examination while handing-over to the relief man. The A4 had to be detached, and an A3, No 2595 *Trigo*, was commandeered at a moment's notice. Driver Nash and Fireman Gilbey of Kings Cross were now in charge, and because of the examination and the changing of engines they left Newcastle eight minutes late. By magnificent running they actually passed Retford on time, having covered the first 129·7 miles from Newcastle in 120½ minutes. Then, despite two slacks for permanent way work that cost about 5 minutes between them, the remaining 138·6 miles to Kings Cross took only 109½ minutes, a total of 230 minutes from Newcastle.

In these emergency conditions therefore, with a train load heavier by nearly 34 per cent, the record of *Papyrus* was lowered by some two minutes. Unfortunately no precise record was taken of the running in the form of a fully detailed log; but in view of its exceptional nature the details contained in the guard's journal were carefully examined by Sir Nigel Gresley himself and the actual time of 230 minutes and the net time of 225 minutes have been accepted as fully authentic.

As if this check were not enough however the circumstances were virtually repeated two days later, except that in this latter case Driver Nash and his mate had some prior warning. The failure of the booked engine was this time advised some little time before the train reached Newcastle. This time they were given one of the final batch of A3s as a substitute, No 2507 *Singapore*, and were able to do something by way of preparation before they actually took over. This time they left Newcastle 34 minutes late, and while there was no chance of recovering so substantial an arrear another sterling effort was made. Kings Cross was reached in an actual time of 227½ minutes – an absolute record; allowing for the effect of the same two checks that had been experienced two days earlier the net time was only 222½ minutes, a truly heroic effort.

I can now tell of an amusing sidelight on the happenings of that particular week. The brake trials with the high-speed trains to which I referred in Chapter Nine of this book were reaching their final stages by the spring of 1939. Many matters of high policy were under discussion, and one day it happened that my old chief, Captain Bernard H. Peter, Managing Director of the Westinghouse Brake and Signal Company, was engaged in some very private discussions with Sir Nigel Gresley when a secretary entered the room and handed the latter a short memorandum. Sir Nigel excused himself for a moment while he read the paper, and then a broad smile spread across his face. It was the report of *Singapore*'s run, following only two days after that of *Trigo*. He tossed the memorandum across to his visitor saying: 'There you are, Peter; any of my damned engines can do the job, whether they have a tin case on or not!'

At the same time one must not gloss over the fact that these magnificent A3 performances would not have been called for had not *two* other Gresley Pacifics fallen down on the job. What the causes of the failures of the two successive A4s were I do not know; but this is not primarily a book about locomotive performance in its widest sense, and it is with the record set up by *Singapore* rather than with the circumstances that preceded it that we are concerned. A net average speed of 72·5mph from Newcastle to Kings Cross with a 290 ton load is a record and achievement of the first magnitude.

During all this period of northern activity the Great Western Railway had remained somewhat in the background, and yet the potentialities for record-breaking remained much the same if not greater. The introduction of the Bristolian express in 1935 seemed to enhance the opportunities. If the four-cylinder 4-6-0 locomotives could attain speeds of over 90mph on the almost level stretch of line between Swindon and Paddington, what more could they do on the long, beautifully aligned 1 in 300 descent from Badminton to Little Somerford, to say nothing of the 1 in 100 banks between Wootton Bassett and Bath on the westbound run of the Bristolian? Nevertheless, although a large number of runs on the Bristolian were logged in both directions of running, no record of a three-figure maximum was secured, either from a King or a Castle class locomotive. Dauntsey bank was rather too short, although one or two of the more enterprising Old Oak drivers got speeds of 97 or 98mph at its foot. Equally, the 1 in 100 descent through Box Tunnel is not exactly an ideal place for making speed records. A tunnel, especially when there is a moderate reverse curve at its exit, does impose an inherent restraint, even though there is one recorded instance of a maximum of 98mph in the depths of the Severn Tunnel!

The Badminton descent, though so favourable for a study of the gradient profile, has some points of similarity to the Stoke bank on the LNER when it comes to the making of maximum speed records. The engine of the up Bristolian was starting cold, and had immediately after starting to surmount the 1 in 75 of Filton incline. Any attempt at heavy initial pounding could cause serious derangement of the firebed, and lead to bad steaming for much of the rest of the journey, and drivers were inclined to nurse their engines up to Filton, and not to press them unduly on the long subsequent ascent at 1 in 300 to Badminton. In this way it was unusual for the summit point to be passed at much more than 65mph. After that there were many instances of maximum speeds between 90 and 95mph at Little Somerford; but it was not until the post-war revival from 1954 onwards that certain deliberate attempts were made to get something higher in this locality.

At the same time Swindon tradition has it that speeds of 100mph were common enough in pre-war days when newly repaired engines were being taken trial trip before being returned to ordinary traffic. When he was Locomotive Works Manager R. A. G. Hannington used to take all the Kings trial trip personally, and so far as he was concerned this meant a run to Didcot and 100mph on the return to Swindon, running light engine. Ample preparation was made to ensure a clear road on these occasions, and the signalmen concerned knew what to expect as these engines came flying through Challow and Uffington doing their ton. It was not always so. There is a story of earlier days, which may possibly have improved in the telling, of how C. B. Collett was carrying out a similar high-speed exploit on the Badminton line. One of the signalmen having accepted a light engine on his block instrument was astonished at the terrific speed of its approach, and catching sight of a bowler-hatted figure on the footplate as the engine shot by, telephoned ahead to have the engine stopped at all costs because it was running away in charge of an escaped lunatic!

Great Western pride of achievement in high-speed running was still smarting under the rather clumsy and partisan attempts to debunk the *City of Truro* exploit of May 1904 that had been made in the *Railway Magazine* in 1934 and 1935, and the thoughts of a group of enthusiasts turned to ways and means of establishing a modern 100mph record. The co-operation of the drivers on the Bristolian was ready enough, but for reasons previously mentioned the conditions never seemed ideal for making the attempt. I need not dwell in detail on how the co-operation of certain Worcester drivers was secured for an attempt down the Honeybourne bank, other than to say that it was not unconnected with the great enthusiasm of certain young gentlemen who were then in residence at Oxford University. Gradient-wise, the Honeybourne bank is ideal, with $4\frac{1}{2}$ miles continuously at 1 in 100 from Campden Tunnel down into the Vale of Evesham; the line is virtually straight, and has the great advantage of a continuing good alignment on gradually easing gradients after the foot of the bank itself is attained. In 1939 the 12.45pm express from Paddington was booked non-stop over the 35·8 miles from Kingham to Worcester in 38 minutes. In view of the generally favourable nature of the road this was not a very exacting schedule; but the loads were light, and the stud of Castle class engines at Worcester maintained in excellent condition.

The young enthusiasts at Oxford, having chatted up certain of the drivers, very wisely sought the co-operation of their great friend and mentor, the veteran train-timer R. E. Charlewood, when it was known that one of the most sporting of the Worcester men was going to make a definite attempt to get the hundred. Tidball was the man, and he worked gradually up to his final and successful attempt. On the first occasion, with engine No 5063 *Earl Baldwin*, the speed was $97\frac{1}{2}$mph; then with No 5049 *Earl of Plymouth* he reached only 95mph. Finally, on 31 July 1939, with engine No 4086 *Builth Castle* and a load of 255 tons behind the tender, the train passed over the crest of the bank at 67mph. Subsequent miles were covered at average speeds of 70, $81\frac{3}{4}$, $85\frac{3}{4}$, $92\frac{1}{4}$, 100, $97\frac{1}{4}$, $94\frac{3}{4}$, and $94\frac{3}{4}$mph. The maximum of 100mph was sustained over a full mile, and confirmed by the stop-watch readings of independent observers. The acceleration down the 1 in 100 gradient was thus continuous and rapid, with successive increments of $11\frac{3}{4}$, 4, $6\frac{1}{2}$, and $7\frac{3}{4}$mph until the foot of the gradient was reached. From this it seems clear that after the first leap from 70 to $81\frac{3}{4}$mph the engine would, if left to itself, have produced the usual Castle maximum of around 90mph at the foot of the bank; but that some considerable inducement was given after the first two miles. The fact that the final increments were $6\frac{1}{2}$ and then

7¾mph suggests that further opening out of the engine was taking place at these very high speeds, and that a prolongation of the gradient would have seen a considerably higher maximum than 100mph. Just before the outbreak of war, therefore, there was secured the first fully authenticated maximum speed of 100mph with a Great Western 4-6-0 locomotive. There were to be many more from 1954 onwards.

On the LMS the spectacular achievements of the Pacifics naturally tended to overshadow the accomplishments of all other engines. Nevertheless the standard of express train running all over the system, which underwent a positive metamorphosis in the last few years before the outbreak of World War II, was founded on the splendid performance characteristics of the two classes of Stanier 4-6-0, both of which proved extremely free-running, as well as strong in acceleration and in climbing the banks. The ever-famous Black Fives were, in relation to their coupled wheel diameter, even faster engines than the Jubilees, and maximum speeds of 91–2mph were attained by these 6ft 4-6-0s. So far as I know an engine of the class was never pressed in an attempt to ascertain the maximum it could attain; but I shall always remember the relative ease with which a shockingly rundown member of the class gave me a maximum of 88mph on the final descent into Nottingham with the Thames–Forth Express. The maximum I have seen recorded with the Jubilees is 95mph, on a very fast run over the Midland line when the 99·1 miles from Leicester to St Pancras were covered in a net time of 84½ minutes. The maximum speeds were successively 89 at East Langton, 93 before Kettering, 93 down Sharnbrook bank, 95 at Radlett, and finally 91mph at Hendon.

So far as I can trace no one ever set out to create a superspeed record with one of the lesser LMS locomotives, in the same way as the various Gresley Pacifics were driven pellmell down the Stoke bank, or the carefully built-up effort of the Worcester drivers was contrived on the 12.45pm express from Paddington. If the LMS had been seriously out for a speed record with its 4-6-0 locomotives the long descent from Blea Moor to Settle Junction would have provided an ideal terrain. It was usual to ease the speed a little round the curves between Helwith Bridge and Stainforth; but the curvature was minimal compared with certain other sections where high speed is regularly run. I shall never forget the winter's night when an ex-LNWR Claughton was allowed to accelerate unhindered for the first few miles downhill from Blea Moor and swept up to 88mph before we were barely out of sight of Ribblehead station! I have many times wondered what might not have been attained, somewhere around Settle, if a Jubilee or even a Claughton had been allowed to continue without hindrance from Blea Moor to Settle Junction, let alone with the inducement given to *Builth Castle* in the descent from Campden Tunnel to Honeybourne on 31 July 1939. The Locomotive Department of the LMS confirmed to me that their dynamometer car records include a maximum speed of 98mph by one of the original Royal Scots, but apart from this near approach, when war came again in September 1939, and with it the end of all opportunities for exceptionally fast running, only the Coronations among LMS express locomotives had been authentically recorded at more than 100mph.

CHAPTER TWELVE

FINAL BOW OF STEAM

THE UNPRECEDENTED strains to which the railways of Great Britain were subjected during World War II left a trail of flotsam and jetsam that penetrated into almost every area and every facet of working in the entire system. Standards of track maintenance deteriorated to the extent that express locomotives of the highest reputation were derailed on plain, straight line; engines failed through shortage of steam, using imported American coal – in South Wales of all places! While such incidents were exceptional, circumstances as a whole did not favour the slightest return towards pre-war standards of speed for many years after the overthrow of Nazi Germany. Furthermore, the management of the British railways was dogged and bedevilled by the many cross-currents of national and international politics, and the railways became engulfed in the turgid flow of austerity that spread so inexorably into so many of our great national institutions. There is no need for me to enlarge here upon the disruptive effect of the nationalisation of the railways from January 1948 upon policies long established by the former independent railway companies, nor of the stultifying effect of the controls and restrictions imposed by government decree, and of the many muddles arising from them. It is enough to note here that railway progress so far as speed of service was concerned was retrograde rather than forward-looking for at least six years after the end of hostilities in Europe.

The first evidence of any railway move from the slough of austerity was to be seen in 1951, when the first new locomotives of national design took the road, and titles were bestowed on a number of hitherto unnamed trains, in association with the Festival of Britain staged during the summer of that year. It was perhaps ironic that R. A. Riddles, who had done so much to advance the prowess and speedworthiness of the steam locomotive in pre-war years, should have had to attune the policy of the nationalised railways to a state of continuing austerity, and when newer forms of traction were having their virtues so extensively publicised should have had to state plainly that his decision to continue with steam was governed by the simple fact that it was the form of traction that provided the most tractive effort per pound sterling. The new locomotives were designed not so much to take advantage of the many techniques that had been introduced since 1939, but to be as trouble-free as possible and to need the minimum of attention on the sheds. That they proved fast and efficient in traffic was a great credit to all concerned in their design and construction; but neither the schedules nor the running conditions favoured the making of new speed records.

In the middle of the war, and in the highly unpropitious circumstances that developed immediately after it was over, the Southern Railway had introduced a new locomotive type that soon had every appearance of being a record-breaker. O. V. S. Bulleid was not the man to be deterred by adverse circumstances; in fact he always accepted them as a challenge. And it was in this spirit that he obtained authority to build the first of his revolutionary Merchant Navy class Pacifics in the middle of the war. Very cleverly they were designated 'mixed traffic', and could therefore be accepted as a contribution to the war effort. Photographs were widely circulated of them hauling heavy goods trains. One can be very sure however that such duties were furthest from Bulleid's mind as the ultimate utilisation of these remarkable locomotives. Of course they were designed as a high-speed express passenger job, and the production of a first batch during the war gave much valuable experience in the day-to-day working of their many novel features. So far as ordinary service was concerned they and their post-war successors of the West Country class were severely handicapped by the relatively slow-scheduled speeds of the immediate post-war years, and by the condition of much of the track, which made high maximum speeds very undesirable. This however did not deter Bulleid from carrying out a number of trials to test the maximum capacity of his new locomotives; and although these trials did not result in any new records of maximum speed they certainly established some new records of end-to-end times over main routes of the Southern Railway.

Mr Bulleid allowed to be published details of some very hard runs between Exeter and Salisbury, Waterloo and Bournemouth, and Victoria and Dover. In view of the records made in the past it was perhaps surprising that nothing of a similar kind was attempted between Salisbury and Waterloo. It is possible that some runs were made, but that the results were not of sufficient consequence to be published. In August 1945 a test was made with a load of 460 tons on the principal boat-train route. A special schedule of 90 minutes had been laid down for the 78 mile run to Dover Marine; but the driver was instructed to go as hard as he could. As a result of passing Orpington more than 5 minutes early he was involved in signal checks between there and Sevenoaks, and took 32 minutes to the latter station, 23·3 miles, yet even so still 4 minutes early. A clear road was obtained between Paddock Wood and Westenhanger, and a fine average speed of 80·8mph maintained over the 21 miles from Marden to Smeeth. There were more checks in conclusion, but even so Dover was reached five minutes inside the special schedule. The maximum speed attained was 86mph.

The Bournemouth run, for which a non-stop schedule of 116 minutes had been laid down for the journey of 107·9 miles, was primarily a test of haulage capacity. A load of no less than 517 tons tare was conveyed and the principal feature of this run was the way in which this load was taken on level and slightly adverse gradients. While this was not exceptional by pre-war standards on the northern lines and by the King class on the Great Western, speeds of 70mph and slightly over in such conditions were certainly exhilarating in the immediate post-war years. No speed exceeding 80mph was attained on the long straight descent from Litchfield Tunnel to Eastleigh. If the Southern had ever seriously thought of competing for the world speed record this magnificently aligned stretch of nearly 20 miles, uniformly inclined downhill at 1 in 250, would have seemed ideal for the attempt; but in footplate experience extending over a number of years the condition of the permanent way did not appear to be in a fit state to carry speeds of much over 80mph. It is of course another matter now, with electrification. Perhaps if nationalisation had not taken place and Bulleid had continued as Chief Mechanical Engineer of the Southern an attempt might have been made. There is no doubt that the Merchant Navy class engines in their original condition were exceptionally free running.

This capacity was amply shown in the tests Bulleid conducted on the Salisbury–Exeter line. Details were published of two runs, one non-stop from Exeter to Salisbury, and the second on a train stopping intermediately at Yeovil Junction. Unlike the tests previously referred to, these two runs were made on revenue-earning as distinct from special trains. The first, worked by engine No 21C14 *Nederland Line* hauling a gross load of 415 tons, gave the fastest time on record over the 88 miles between Exeter and Salisbury, namely 86min 6sec; but this time included the effect of two signal checks, and the net time did not exceed 81½ minutes, an average speed over this hilly route of 64·8mph. The chief merit of the run lay however in the uphill performance, and apart from the overall time no speed records of any kind were involved. On the second journey, however, with engine No 21C13 *Blue Funnel Line* and a ten-coach train of 345 tons gross, some very fast running was made, including a maximum of 96mph down the bank from Honiton Tunnel to Seaton Junction. In the record start-to-stop time of 44min 14sec for the 48·9 miles from Exeter to Yeovil Junction (66·3mph) was included the high average of 78·2mph over the 28·5 miles from Honiton Tunnel West End to Sutton Bingham. The second stage of this run, from Yeovil Junction to Salisbury, was spoiled by two permanent-way checks. Despite the peculiar failures that occurred all too frequently from novel features in the design of these locomotives it seemed clear that the Merchant Navy class were potential record breakers. Unfortunately circumstances supervened to preclude any opportunities that may have come their way.

After the new mechanical engineering organisation of the nationalised railways had settled into its stride the principal concern became that of re-establishing pre-war standards of performance on post-war fuel, and the problems were mainly those of heavy load haulage at speeds of 60 to 65mph rather than the operation of medium express trains at really high speed. Viewing the period in retrospect and commenting upon the shortsightedness of management rather than any shortcomings of technical engineering ability, it is truly astonishing that the sales value of high speed was so little appreciated at the time. As recently as the year 1962 I remember hearing with alarm that no appreciable acceleration of service had been contemplated when the electrification from Euston to Liverpool and Manchester was completed. Such an attitude can only be placed on the same pedestal of folly as that which used glibly to assert that the financial troubles of the nationalised railways would vanish overnight once we had got rid of steam traction! Fortunately there were gallant spirits in some of the regions who saw that the way to passenger business was through acceleration of service, and who had sufficient freedom of action left to be able to carry their precepts into operation. But before coming to describe the results of the enterprise which restored full pre-war speed on the Western Region and which led up to new records of high-speed running by both Castle and King class locomotives, I must refer to a new form of record that was achieved by the Gresley A4 Pacifics in the late summer of 1948.

On the afternoon of 12 August that year, storms of unprecedented violence swept over south-eastern Scotland. The floodwater cascading down from the hills washed away no fewer than seven bridges on the East Coast main line between Berwick and Dunbar; it caused breaches by three major landslips, and brought a critical danger to the countryside near Ayton, where the high railway embankment acted as a dam, and was at one time feared to be on the point of collapsing and allowing a vast volume of flood-water to inundate the whole country seawards of the railway. In that summer the Flying Scotsman was once again running non-stop between Kings Cross and Edinburgh; but with this multiple breaching of the line north of Berwick, which could not be repaired for many months, diversion of the non-stop and all other East Coast trains was necessary. They took the left hand turn at Tweedmouth, and travelled via Kelso to St Boswell's, whence they proceeded on the Waverley route to Edinburgh. This diversion increased the distance between London and Edinburgh traversed by these trains from 392·7 miles to 408·6, and at first the idea of maintaining the non-stop run was not in anyone's mind. It was not so much the extra 16 miles of journey as the exceptional difficulty of the Waverley route between Edinburgh and Galashiels. The long climb to Falahill meant heavy consumption of coal and water, and then spinning out the water supply until Lucker troughs were reached, 90 miles from Edinburgh. Nevertheless, although conditions were not greatly improved from the austerity of wartime there were some very keen drivers in the top link at Haymarket shed, and no more than twelve days after the flood disaster one of these worthies decided to have a go.

With No 60029 *Woodcock* Driver Stevenson nursed the engine so skilfully on the long climb to Falahill that he judged he had enough water to get through to Lucker without making the provisional stop at Galashiels to replenish the tender. After leaving the Waverley route at St Boswell's the connecting line down the Tweed valley, through Kelso, was subject to severely restricted speed, and involved no appreciable consumption of water or coal. He succeeded in getting comfortably through to Lucker and on this day, 24 August 1948, for the first time the Flying Scotsman was run non-stop from Edinburgh to Kings Cross via Galashiels. This was a new record non-stop run of 408·6 miles for this country. The speed was not heroic, but the prestige of running non-stop between the two capital cities in such conditions was immense. Between that date and the end of the summer service the non-stop run was made on no fewer than eight occasions northbound, and nine times southbound. It is worth recalling the engines concerned, as some of them have previously featured in this story of record breaking.

Northbound:	
Woodcock	four times
Sea Eagle	once each
Merlin	
Golden Plover	
Commonwealth of Australia	
Southbound:	
Woodcock	five times
Commonwealth of Australia	twice
Sea Eagle	once each
Mallard	

In later years the schedule of the summer non-stop was gradually reduced till in 1954 it was no more thaan 6½ hours involving an overall average speed of 60·4mph. It remained the world's record non-stop run with steam, and that fast overall time did not represent the maximum of which the A4 engines were capable. On-time arrivals after delays of 10 to 15 minutes en route were quite frequent. I have not been able to ascertain the fastest end-to-end time ever made, but a journey of my own provided a net gain of no less than 21 minutes on schedule; 369min for the 392·7 miles, and an average speed of 63·8mph.

Turning now to the Western Region, we find that the acceleration of the Bristolian to its pre-war timing of 1¾ hours between Paddington and Bristol was the centre-piece of a remarkable resurgence of high-speed running on many routes of the former Great Western Railway. It needed all the resolution of the top management of the Region to bring these accelerations into effect, because several very senior officers had become so reconciled to the difficulties of post-war operation as to be convinced that such accelerations were impracticable with the motive power then available. It was perhaps understandable that non-technical men should have doubts of the continuing capacity of locomotive designs introduced in 1923 and 1927 to meet such severe requirements in the conditions prevailing in the 1950s; but fortunately the determination of the General Manager, K. W. C. Grand, was matched by the new-found drive and enthusiasm in the locomotive works at Swindon, then under the direction of R. A. Smeddle. The story of how Castle and King class locomotives were modernised has been told in full detail in my book *The Stars, Castles and Kings of the GWR*: it is necessary here to tell only of their achievements on the road.

In pre-war years, as related in the previous chapter, it was only after a good deal of preparation – albeit unofficial – that a record of 100mph was obtained with one of these engines. In the exhilarating revival that took place from 1953 onwards the emphasis tended to move to the King rather than the Castle class locomotive. It is not always appreciated that on theoretical grounds the Kings were potentially the faster engines, with piston valves larger in proportion to the cylinder volume and thus permitting of a freer exhaust. The fact that the Kings were taken off the Bristolian after a relatively short period was taken by some commentators to suggest that these engines were not so suitable for sustained high speed running as the Castles. This, of course, was not the case. It was simply that the Castles were found amply capable of doing the job, and that the Kings could be better employed on the heavy West of England and Birmingham trains, many of which, in pre-war years, were definitely beyond the capacity of a Castle.

The preparations for renewed high-speed running on the Western Region extended far beyond the modernising of the four-cylinder 4-6-0 locomotives. A great deal of work was done on the track to permit of continuous running at 85 to 90mph, while on certain sections of line that were in particularly good condition the Chief Civil Engineer took the unprecedented step of removing the top limit of speed altogether. The working timetables listed certain stretches over which, to quote, 'the speed may be as high as necessary'. If there had ever been an inviation to the more enterprising of the drivers to have a go this was it! From the later nineteen thirties speedometers had been fitted to all the first-line express passenger locomotives. It was a very simple device, consisting of a small alternating-current generator driven direct from the rearmost driving wheel, and a voltmeter in the cab that was graduated to read in miles per hour. In my own footplate experience they were usually fairly accurate, but naturally had not the precision of the integrator table in the dynamometer car, or yet of an accurate stop watch in experienced hands. But the presence of that simple and invaluable instrument just in front of the driver and the lifting of all speed restriction on such tempting stretches of line as the Lavington bank, the descent to Curry Rivel Junction, Wellington bank, and lengthy stretches of the Bristol main line led to some exciting pieces of running. There were frequent reports from drivers and running inspectors of maximum speeds of 100mph and more with Castle class engines between Badminton and Little Somerford, though in actual fact only one authenticated record, from an independent observer in the train, has been secured. This maximum formed part of a new record for the Bristol–Paddington which will be referred to in detail later.

At this stage some considerable discussion took place among Western Region men as to the relative merits for maximum-speed running of the original Castle class engines with low superheat and sight-feed hydrostatic lubricators, and the medium-superheat Hawksworth engines with mechanical lubricators. There is no doubt that in good steaming conditions the majority of the drivers preferrred the older engines, on which they could regulate the oil supply. It is true that the higher degree of superheat gave them a better chance with inferior fuel, but this was a case of making ordinary speed, rather than breaking maximum-speed records. It was another matter with the high superheat engines of later years. The Kings of course never went through the medium-superheat stage. Hawksworth himself modified No 6022, and greatly increased her reliability, with post-war qualities of coal; and when Smeddle sponsored the alteration to the draughting, a number of Kings were fitted with four-row superheaters. It was one of these engines that gave the first fully authenticated record of more than 100mph, equalling the fifty-year-old claim for 102·3mph for the *City of Truro*. I was a passenger on the down Bristolian on the day in question, and logged the run in full detail.

We had the usual seven-coach load, 236 tons tare, and about 250 tons full, with engine No 6018 *King Henry VI*: Driver Pithers and Fireman French of Old Oak shed. It was a calm and fine summer's day, and despite two permanent-way checks the train passed Swindon slightly ahead of time. There was a representative of the Chief Civil Engineer riding on the footplate and the effort that followed was probably made for test purposes, though no undue pressing of the locomotive was needed to achieve it. On page 194 is an extract from the log over the critical stage of the journey.

When the Castles replaced the Kings on the Bristolian the locomotive working was changed. The London engine that had come down on the 8.45am from Paddington returned on the 12 noon up express, instead of waiting all day at Bristol

Distance from Paddington miles		Time from Paddington min sec	Speeds mph
73·8	*Marston East Box*	62 01	50*
77·3	SWINDON	65 31	69
80·0	*Hay Lane Box*	67 38	79
82·9	Wootton Bassett	69 44	85
84·0	*Milepost 84*	70 30	88
85·0	,, *85*	71 11	89
86·0	,, *86*	71 50	95
87·0	,, *87*	72 27	102½
87¾	Dauntsey	72 53½	—
89·0	*Milepost 89*	73 39	98
90·0	,, *90*	74 16	95
91·0	,, *91*	74 55	91½
—		eased	—
94·0	CHIPPENHAM	77 00	80

* recovering from speed restriction
Average speed Mileposts 87–9 = 100 mph

for the up flyer. The latter was then worked by a Bristol engine, which returned on the 7.50pm from Paddington. The record time for the run, in either direction, was made by the four-row superheater Castle class engine No 7018 *Drysllwyn Castle*, fitted also with a twin-orifice blastpipe and chimney. This run was made at a time when acceleration to a schedule of 100 minutes in each direction was contemplated, and the engine was worked a bit heavy to see how much time was in hand. With a gross load of 260 tons behind the tender the result was an overall time of 93min 50sec, a start-to-stop average speed of 75·4mph. The road was clear throughout, and it was on this trip that a maximum speed of 100mph was attained at Little Somerford. The fast overall time was achieved principally as a result of a start much harder than usual from Bristol, with speed worked up to no less than 73mph on the long rise to Badminton. On the long-sustained high-speed stretch between Shrivenham and Goring, 26·8 miles, the average speed of 87·9mph was beaten on no less than two occasions when I was on the footplate: once with the same engine, when the average was 88·8mph, and secondly with a low-superheat engine No 5076 *Gladiator*, with 88·6mph. These two occasions however gave times of between two and three minutes longer between Bristol and Swindon. An even faster net time was recorded on the down journey, when an additional load of nine coaches, 279 tons tare, 300 tons full was worked by engine No 6015 *King Richard III*. That engine had been fitted with twin-orifice blastpipe and chimney, and was an exceptionally fast machine. Severe delays beset the path of the Bristolian on this occasion, and although some notably vigorous running was made the total time from Paddington to Temple Meads was 109min 24sec. The net time however did not exceed 92 minutes – a remarkable average, with a 300-ton train, of 76·8mph. The maximum down the Dauntsey incline was 98mph.

When this engine was newly equipped with a double chimney great interest was displayed in her prowess by the Chief Mechanical Engineer's department at Swindon; and in my book *Stars, Castles and Kings of the GWR, Part II* I have described in detail how a very high maximum speed was obtained in descending the Lavington bank with the Cornish Riviera Express. Two alternate quarter miles were clocked at 106½ and 108½mph, and the average speed over three quarters of a mile was 107½mph. This, so far as can be ascertained, is the highest burst of speed to be credited to any British steam locomotive other than the Gresley A3 and A4 Pacifics and the Stanier Duchess class. It was unfortunately the subject of some exaggeration in some popular press reports, one quoting as much as 116mph. Careful examination of the evidence of the *two* observers present on the footplate on this occasion is enough to establish a speed of 108mph as the record for the double-chimneyed King class.

The fitting of double-chimneys to many of the Castles

definitely enhanced their maximum speed abilities, though the utmost that has been authentically recorded is 103mph. The engine concerned was No 7030 *Cranbrook Castle*, with a light load of 108 tons, in the course of some test runs on the Birmingham line in 1962. The maximum speed was twice achieved, first at Blackthorn, and then at Denham. Careful observance of the various permanent speed restrictions however precluded any faster start-to-stop time than 51min 59sec for the 60·8 miles from Leamington to High Wycombe. Towards the end of the steam era no great new records were made in the realm of either start-to-stop averages or maximum speed, but mention must be made of three more locomotive classes that are fully documented as crossing the magic 100mph line. All were Pacifics, two ex-LNER and one Southern. The three cases were:

Region	*Engine*		*Class*	*Max speed mph*	*Location*
	No	*Name*			
Eastern	60133	*Pommern*	A1	102	Essendine
Eastern	60526	*Sugar Plum*	A2	102	Essendine
Southern	35028	*Clan Line*	MN	104	Axminster

In the last weeks of steam traction on the Bournemouth certain of the more sporting of the drivers were making very hard runs east of Basingstoke in satisfying their own ego and delighting many amateur enthusiasts. Several instances were claimed of speeds of more than 100mph, but nothing to surpass the performance of *Clan Line* on the late lamented Atlantic Coast Express seems to have been fully authenticated.

In coming to the end of the steam era, and with it the end of this book, one cannot refrain from speculating as to what might have been achieved had a definite and closely regulated speed contest been staged. I once went so far as to suggest that the Stoke–Werrington section of the East Coast main line might be used for such a demonstration, and that if British Railways had cared to run excursions to witness the trials the demand for seats would have been such as to outweigh by far the cost of making the tests. I also suggested that the test trains should be started from further afield than the Barkston triangle! It would have been highly interesting to see how an original Merchant Navy, in the pink of condition, and a Duchess class Pacific would have fared against a Gresley A4 if driven with the same determination as that exercised on the classic run of *Mallard*. In mentioning those two designs I have perhaps named what I consider to have been the most likely challengers of LNER supremacy. It was however not likely that my slight hint would be taken up, and so far as authenticated records go the final order, in the speed range of 100mph and over, stands as follows:

LNER	A4 Pacific	126 mph
LMS	Coronation Pacific	114 mph
GWR	Double-chimneyed King	108 mph
LNER	A3 Pacific	108 mph
SR	Rebuilt Merchant Navy	104 mph
GWR	Double-chimneyed Castle	103 mph
LNER	A1 Pacific	102 mph
LNER	A2 Pacific	102 mph

Finally, there are the probable hundreds, by *Flying Scotsman* on the Leeds experimental run of November 1934, and by *City of Truro* on 9 May 1904. What might have been, in other directions, is still a source of constant debate. In the foregoing list I have not included the single-chimneyed records of both Kings and Castles, which stand at 102½ and 100mph, nor those of the non-streamlined Duchess class Pacifics of the LMS. The latter engines were no less swift than the streamlined pioneers of the class, and a record of 105mph at the foot of Beattock was made by the *City of Nottingham*.

Now all this is at an end. It is a time when preparations

are being made in many parts of the world for still faster trains. A speed of more than 200mph has already been attained by a French electrically hauled train; plans are being made for British trains to run at more than 125mph regularly on our crowded main lines. All this is thoroughly in keeping with the times, and we can look forward to a new era of record breaking, with the motive power of today and tomorrow. Whatever is achieved, however, nothing is likely to lessen the interest and intense respect that railway enthusiasts will always have for the achievements of the steam age on the railways of Great Britain.

APPENDIX

CITY OF TRURO: 102·3MPH?

THE FOLLOWING is an attempted reconstruction of what actually happened in the descent of Wellington bank, using as much as possible of Rous-Marten's original data. The speed at Whiteball summit was about 52mph and then from Milepost 173 onwards every quarter mile was clocked, using two stop watches, starting one and stopping the other alternatively. These readings gave speeds of 81·8, 84·9, 88·2, 90·0, 91·8, 95·7, 97·8, and 102.3mph. On a plotted graph these speeds lie on a perfectly reasonable and fair curve, except the last. I am quite prepared to believe that Rous-Marten may have been one-fifth of a second out on the final reading, getting 102·3 instead of the level 100mph. Then came the check, resulting from some platelayers remaining perilously late in the track of the mail train. Rous-Marten, as usual, told a highly colourful story of how they loafed in the four-foot until the very last minute, despite prolonged whistling of the engine; but a first-class driver must have known that no application of the brakes at the last minute could possibly have saved the men had they persisted in remaining on the line.

I feel it is much more likely that the driver, realising the terrific speed at which he was travelling, shut off steam deliberately and eased the train over the reverse curves through Wellington station. A heavy brake application with the apparatus then in use would have brought speed down to about 64mph through Wellington station. In previous discussions on this episode there has been more than a suggestion that those on the footplate were going for an all-out record. As previously explained in Chapter Six of this book the speeds between Exeter and Whiteball hardly bear out this where the times of *City of Truro* were substantially beaten by the *City of Exeter* on an earlier Ocean Mail run. I feel that the *City of Truro* was not specially pressed from Whiteball but simply allowed to run, probably with little change in the working conditions, and that the very high speed was an incidental feature, like that of *Silver Link* in 1935, rather than a deliberate attempt at a world record.

The one major item published by Rous-Marten that does not fit in with the reconstruction I have attempted is the passing time at Wellington station. However, in many years of speed recording personally, now amounting to near fifty, I have found it is extremely easy to jot down a station time 20 or 30 seconds out. When times are subsequently checked against speeds the error readily comes to light; but in the case of the *City of Truro* run so strict a censorship had been imposed upon the speeds that in the original published records it is probable that no exhaustive check was made. If the passing time at Wellington is adjusted from 3min 7sec after Whiteball to 2 min 47sec all the other details fall into place.

In his first published account of the run in the *Railway Magazine* for June 1904 Rous-Marten says that the check occurred near Wellington station, and in my reconstruction the lowest speed due to the brake application occurred about a quarter of a mile after passing the station, this corresponding with a note in a log published in *The Engineer* at the time. In the discussion that took place in the *Railway Magazine* of 1934 and 1935 some confusion was caused by reference to a letter to *The Times* written by Locomotive Inspector Flewellyn many years after the event in which he stated that speed was reduced near Bradfield Crossing – that is, about half-way between Wellington and Norton Fitzwarren stations. This is however so much at variance with every other account of the trip that I feel it must be discounted. Although we shall never know precisely what happened, my own conviction is that with the one exception of the time at Wellington station Rous-Marten's published figures were accurate. I feel that a maximum speed of at least 100mph may be accepted on *City of Truro*'s behalf.

INDEX

Illustrations are indicated by bold type

ENGINEERS

LOCOMOTIVES, INDIVIDUAL

LOCOMOTIVE TYPES

RECORDERS

RUNS

Regional History and David & Charles Series